TRUTH ABOUT EVOLUTION AND THE BIBLE

TEACHINGS OF
THE ORDER OF CHRISTIAN MYSTICS

THE TRUTH ABOUT EVOLUTION AND THE BIBLE

TEACHINGS OF THE ORDER OF CHRISTIAN MYSTICS

THE "CURTISS BOOKS" FREELY AVAILABLE AT

WWW.ORDEROFCHRISTIANMYSTICS.CO.ZA

1. THE VOICE OF ISIS
2. THE MESSAGE OF AQUARIA
3. THE INNER RADIANCE
4. REALMS OF THE LIVING DEAD
5. COMING WORLD CHANGES
6. THE KEY TO THE UNIVERSE
7. THE KEY OF DESTINY
8. LETTERS FROM THE TEACHER VOLUME I
9. LETTERS FROM THE TEACHER VOLUME II
10. THE TRUTH ABOUT EVOLUTION AND THE BIBLE
11. THE PHILOSOPHY OF WAR
12. PERSONAL SURVIVAL
13. THE PATTERN LIFE
14. FOUR-FOLD HEALTH
15. VITAMINS
16. WHY ARE WE HERE?
17. REINCARNATION
18. FOR YOUNG SOULS
19. GEMS OF MYSTICISM
20. THE TEMPLE OF SILENCE
21. THE DIVINE MOTHER
22. THE SOUNDLESS SOUND
23. THE MYSTIC LIFE
24. THE LOVE OF RABIACCA
25. POTENT PRAYERS

SUPPORTING VOLUMES

26. THE SEVENTH SEAL
27. TOWARDS THE LIGHT

THE TRUTH ABOUT EVOLUTION AND THE BIBLE

Transcribed by
HARRIETTE AUGUSTA CURTISS
and
F. HOMER CURTISS, B.S., M.D.
Founders of
THE ORDER OF CHRISTIAN MYSTICS
and
AUTHORS OF THE "CURTISS BOOKS"

2012 EDITION

REPUBLISHED FOR THE ORDER BY
MOUNT LINDEN PUBLISHING
JOHANNESBURG, SOUTH AFRICA
ISBN: 978-1-920483-15-9

Dedication

This edition is lovingly dedicated to the Memory

of the Founders of

The Order of Christian Mystics

Pyrahmos and Rahmea

and to

The Teacher of the Order

who on earth was called

Helena Petrovna Blavatsky

"Ministers of Christ and Stewards of the Mysteries of God."
1 Corinthians 4 vs. 1

COPYRIGHT 2012

BY
MOUNT LINDEN PUBLISHING

First Published in 1921

May be used for non-commercial, personal, research and educational use.
ALL RIGHTS RESERVED

CONTENTS

INTRODUCTION
"If we really understand what evolution means, and if we understand what the *Bible* really says as to the origin of man, we will find that there is no conflict between science and religion or between evolution and the Bible, only between misconceptions on both sides." Necessity for aeroplane views of modern conditions. xi

CHAPTER I. *Science*
"Facts and laws, when repeatedly observed, proved and demonstrated, are said to be scientific." Science underlies all our modern civilization, all our creature comforts and all our conceptions of life and the universe in which we live. What science has proved as to the evolution of forms through Embryology, Palaeontology, Anthropology, Comparative Anatomy, etc. 17

CHAPTER II. *Materialism*
Not a sound philosophy. Now replaced by dynamism. Can explain processes but not origins and causes. "The bankruptcy of materialism... is now evident." Accept its facts, but need not accept its conclusions. 25

CHAPTER III. *The Law of Manifestation*
All manifestation from a single cell; from within outward. Necessity of a pattern. How

the pattern is materialized. Why a plant or animal stops growing in size. Meaning of Hebrew word "created." Necessity of a causative factor tending toward a predetermined end. Examples of the conscious actions of cells. 33

CHAPTER IV. *Creation*
Length of the "days" of creation. Geological evidence. "The Lord God made every plant of the field *before it was in the earth*, and every herb of the field *before it grew*." The Adam of the first chapter of Genesis a purely Spiritual Man, in the image and likeness of God. A spiritual and pre-physical being, created not evolved. 46

CHAPTER V. *Creation (Concluded)*
The two Adams. Adam of the second chapter not "created" but "formed" or evolved. The vital difference. Body of man not the offspring of the ape. Why? How? How man became "a living Soul." Paul's testimony as to the conflict between the Spiritual Man and the animal man. What was "the fall of man"? "Original sin"?. 54

CHAPTER VI. *Manifesting the Creation*
Why is the body so imperfect and prone to sickness and disease? Effects of inharmonious creations. Evolution not a mechanical process. Progress requires effort. 66

CHAPTER VII. *Manifesting the Creation (Concluded)*
Change essential to progress. Effect of radium. Spiritual radio-activity. 74

CHAPTER VIII. *Adam and Eve*
   Adam and Eve not the parents of all mankind. How the separation of the sexes took place. Meaning of the rib. Sex inheres in the Soul. Woman's place and duty in society. Reasons for her "inferiority complex," dress fads, cosmetics, "sex appeal". . 81

CHAPTER IX. *The Garden in Eden*
   No such locality ever found. Necessity for another interpretation. Testimony of St Augustine. How long did it take Adam to name 1,000,000 species? Meaning of the four rivers. Difference between Eden and the Garden. How the *Bible* was compiled. The role of inspiration. 94

CHAPTER X. *The Trees in the Garden*
   Hebrew words for Garden and Tree. How justify the Hebrews' seizing of other people's lands? Tree of Knowledge. Tree of Life. *Kundalini-force.* Dangers of eating the fruit. Origin of evil. Why banished from Eden?. 109

CHAPTER XI. *The Serpent Power*
   Serpent not the initiator of evil. Why used as a symbol? Meaning of the word. Sex not impure. Only method of incarnation. Rod of Moses and Aaron. Caduceus. *Kundalini-force.* Effect on spinal cord and brain. 125

CHAPTER XII. *The Serpent Power (Concluded)*
   The curse of the serpent. Fruit of the tree. Adam and Eve not driven from the Garden for using the sex functions. 136

CHAPTER XIII. *Unity in Duality*
   Manifesting the unity of the Soul in the duality

of the sexes. Sex underlies all manifestation. Not merely an animal function. Doctrine of spiritual mates. 142

CHAPTER XIV. *The Twain One Flesh*

Marriage made in heaven. Two expressions of the same Higher Self. Geometrical proof. Object of the Soul's incarnation. Marriage rite essentially spiritual. No satisfaction possible in promiscuity. Wrong mental attitude short-circuits forces. "Risen above sex." No normal woman frigid. Object of marriage. Sex equality, and woman's rights. Trial and companionate marriages. . . . 150

Chapter XV. *Summary*. 168

Supplementary Chapters

CHAPTER XVI. *God. Part I. – The Three-fold Flame – The Father*

Connection with light and fire. Sibylline Oracles. Three persons of the Trinity. God a consuming fire yet a God of Love. Prayer to Divine Mother; Evening Prayer. 175

CHAPTER XVII. *God. Part II. – The Chariot of Fire – The Divine Mother*

The "Sun behind the Sun." Chariot descends periodically. Meaning of "Swing Low, Sweet Chariot." Effect of the "Fire of the Lord.". . . . 189

CHAPTER XVIII *God. Part III. – The Christos – The Son*

Growth of the Christ-seed in man. How to unfold the mind centers. The second coming of the Christ. 201

CHAPTER XIX. *The Image of God*
   The Mill of the Gods. The Wheel of Time. What is the Image? Steps in its manifestation. 215

CHAPTER XX. *Emmanuel*
   Mystic symbology of Jesus' life; meaning of the word virgin; symbology of Mary; meaning of Emmanuel; not a knowledge, but a realization; symbology of blood; mystic symbology of the rainbow. 229

Index
   Elaborated for use of students. 239

EVOLUTION

They quiver, shift and change like human hope,
These myriad forms in the Kaleidoscope,

Abide their little hour and are gone,
As Life's fast flying wheel whirls ever on.

Each flows out from one evolved before
In equal charm, or may be less — or more.

But naught remains unchanged. All things must shift
Into such forms as next may be the gift

Of Him who turns the wheel. Yet see the Law
With certitude serene, infinite, draw

A golden thread forever through the maze
Uniting present, past and future days.

Though men with tints and colors may essay,
They work inside of lines drawn yesterday.

To-morrow shows a scene of woe or weal,
A sequence sure of this day's sloth or zeal.

Thus runs the Law, life's atoms bright arranging,
And combinations new reflect the changing.

Each form has intimate, complete relation
To that just past, its source and derivation.

Learn day by day similitudes to scan;
See in this toy, somewhat the way of man,

From out the Spiritual Sun a Ray,
Held by the magic of the Law in clay.

Who knows what fairest form of all
Shall last – and perfect – on our shoulders fall?

FRED BURBANK LEYNS, *Fellow O.C.M.*
Courtesy of *The Square and Compass,* Denver.

INTRODUCTION

"Get wisdom, get understanding: forget *it* not.... Forsake her not, and she shall preserve thee; love her, and she shall keep thee." *Proverbs*, iv, 5, 6.

"Men who know very little of science and men who know very little of religion do indeed get to quarreling, and the onlookers imagine that there is a conflict between science and religion, whereas the conflict is only between two different species of ignorance." Prof. Robt. A. Millikan, *Collier's*, Oct 24, 1925, 6.

"Wisdom is the principal thing", Solomon tells us. "Therefore get wisdom: and with all thy getting get understanding." If we have a real understanding of a principle we can grasp and comprehend the many seemingly conflicting aspects of its manifestation and thus solve the problems its diverse aspects may present. This is particularly true of the apparent conflict between the doctrine of evolution and the statements of the *Bible* as to the origin of man. For, if we really understand what evolution means, and if we understand what the *Bible* really says as to the origin of man, we will find that there is no conflict between science and religion or between evolution and the *Bible*, only between misconceptions on both sides. Both sides are right in a way, but both are talking about entirely different things.

Since it would require several volumes to expound

and fully corroborate the philosophy presented in this volume, especially its theological implications, and altho many theological card-houses will necessarily be toppled over, because they are built upon the shifting sands of human speculation instead of upon Cosmic Law and the Rock of Eternal Truth, nevertheless, we will have to confine ourselves more to an outline than to a complete exposition of the subject.

In the subsequent pages if we do not give more elaborate corroborative examples and arguments, or if at times we may speak somewhat dogmatically, it should be remembered that only sufficient of the philosophy can be given herein to substantiate our main thesis. We will endeavor, however, to give sufficient illustrations and to point out the same laws working in Nature all about us to convince the average unprejudiced mind that does not have a thesis of its own to modify or discard ere it can grasp a new conception. Those who are studiously inclined will find many of the points more fully elaborated in our other volumes.[1]

To gain a true understanding of any principle or problem we must have, firstly, a willingness to accept truth when it is proved to us, and secondly, we must have minds whose channels of thinking are not fossilized into grooves by traditions which mould and distort every fact according to preconceived conceptions. In other words, not only must we have minds

---

[1] Particularly *The Key to the Universe*, *The Key of Destiny* and *The Voice of Isis*.

that are plastic enough to grasp new ideas, but we must have the willingness to accept new points of view, new conceptions and new truths when they are demonstrated to us. Also we must not permit our emotions—whether religious or of scientific impatience or intellectual contempt—to enter into what should be a calm, rational and scientific examination of the *proved facts* of the case and the *unvarying laws* of Nature back of them. For, if we do, the resulting emotional storm upsets the quiet balance of our reasoning and even of our intuitive faculties, and blinds us to the truth, no matter how unassailably presented, both logically and scientifically. As we have said elsewhere: "It is well to heed the past, yet not to live in it and say that that which has been is all that can ever be, but to reason intelligently from the underlying principles which are the same yesterday, today and forever, altho they find ever greater facilities for more perfect expression as evolution advances. The Tree of Life grows from age to age and puts forth fresh branches and leaves and fruit perhaps undreamed of when it was but a sapling; nevertheless it grows always from the Everlasting Root, and but expresses that which was present altho unmanifested within the seed. And ever it is the same fundamental process of Nature which puts forth its new experiences".[2]

Proved facts are realities, while appearances may be but certain aspects of those facts seen under vary-

---
[2] *The Message of Aquaria*, Curtiss, 25.

ing and often limiting conditions. With the investigations of science and the progress of knowledge, both our understanding and our interpretation of facts must progress and enlarge. New scientific interpretations of facts often require some time for their general acceptance, because of the inertia of the mind and the power of habit or the impetus of former ideas. Yet, because of the willingness, even eagerness, of the truly scientific mind to arrive at the truth, and its willingness to thrash out objections in the open, the period required for the acceptance of new conceptions and new truths in the scientific world is relatively short. But in religious matters the case is far different.

The spiritual realities, the eternal verities, are ever the same. Yet with the advance of knowledge and the expansion of man's consciousness their interpretations should also advance as greater light is shed upon them. However, in the religious field there is not the willingness to face truth and modify old conceptions, even if those old conceptions were interpretations made by a handful of men during the Dark Ages. The minds of a majority in the Christian world today are still shackled and limited by the creeds and dogmas formulated so long ago by their respective churches. They fail to realize that there are no creeds or dogmas in the *Bible*: that all such are but man-made interpretations of certain spiritual truths, made by groups of men as fallible as ourselves in long bygone ages when the knowledge of Nature and her laws was limited: was speculative instead of scientific.

Many religious conceptions today are in much the same class as were the conceptions of science and medicine during the Dark Ages. Since the Fundamentalists are literalists they may be regarded as materialists in religion, failing to recognize that they are living in the age of radium, the radio, television and the aeroplane. They fail to realize that mankind will no longer tolerate the oxcart or the one-horse-chaise interpretations of either scientific or religious truths, but insists on mental and spiritual aeroplanes in which they can rise above the literal, materialistic and earth-plane conceptions of former ages and get an aerial view of the spiritual landscape and so judge as to the relative value of mere appearances.

Yet the Fundamentalists are right in holding to their inner realization that man was created in the image of God and not of an ape. But it depends upon their conception and definition of man.

On the other hand science is right in claiming that all forms of life on Earth—both plant and animal—have evolved gradually from the simplest beginnings, and that these forms have developed—altho not uniformly—through successive stages of complexity until they culminate in man.

Apparently these two ideas are contradictory, diametrically opposed and irreconcilable, and yet in truth they are not. The conflict is only between the respective definitions of man. One refers to the

Spiritual Man and the other to his physical vehicle or body, yet both these two men are distinctly mentioned and accurately described in the *Bible*. It is the failure to make the distinction and discrimination between these two that has caused the confusion and led to the controversy between the two schools of thought. Both are sincere and both stand firmly for their honest convictions, and *both are right* from their point of view. But in both cases their point of view is limited by their lack of understanding of all the facts in the case and to their lack of consideration of the other's viewpoint.

It is just this lack of understanding each of the other which we hope to remedy in this volume by pointing out to both the plain statements of the *Bible* which *support both sides* and thus reconcile all their differences through true understanding and its resulting wisdom.

THE TRUTH ABOUT EVOLUTION AND THE BIBLE

CHAPTER I

SCIENCE

"Evolution is a natural history of the cosmos, including organic beings, expressed in physical terms as a mechanical process." *Encyclopaedia Britannica*, x, 22.

"Anyone who is practically acquainted with scientific work is aware that those who refuse to go beyond fact, rarely get as far as fact." *Collected Essays*, Huxley, i, 62.

"It is not beyond belief that we may sometime be able to do in our laboratories what the Sun is doing in its laboratory. . . . But to what end? Without the moral background of religion, without the spirit of service which is the essence of religion, our new powers will only be the means of our destruction." Prof. Robt. A. Millikan, *Collier's*, Oct 24, 1925, 6.

Science is the handmaiden of religion. But at present she is on a strike, because she will not accept as scientific facts man-made dogmas in which she can find no evidence of facts.

The desire to know and understand is an intellectual manifestation of the Soul's inherent desire for truth. It finds expression in the intellectually awakened thru curiosity—transient or persistent according to the degree of the awakening. The result of such curiosity is a more critical observation of appearances, phenomena and events. And when such observations are organized and studied they lead to the discovery of facts and the laws of manifestation underlying them. Such facts and laws, when repeatedly observed, proved and demonstrated, are said to be scientific. Hence, science has been called organized knowledge: knowledge which can be demonstrated at any appropriate time and place by anyone who complies with the laws involved.

The facts and laws thus discovered and proved by science, especially during the last half century, are truly marvelous, most enlightening and mind-expanding as well as extremely valuable. They underlie all our modern civilization, all our creature comforts and all our conceptions of life and the universe in which we live. Where would we be today, for instance, without the steam and gas engines? Without electricity, the aeroplane, the radio, etc.? And if acceptance of these facts and laws discovered by science is essential to modern civilization and comfort, it is equally essential that we accept other facts which have, just as painstakingly and accurately, been proved by science, even tho we are not as familiar with all the steps of their demonstration. When practically the whole scientific world agrees as to the accuracy of certain clearly demonstrated facts it is but exposing both our ignorance and our mental fossilization, it is assassination of our reasoning faculties, to deny them. We can, however, deny *not the facts*, but certain scientific *interpretations* of them.

SCIENCE

In fact, in the light of new discoveries, the scientific world itself necessarily changes its interpretation of the facts so frequently that its text-books have to be rewritten every few years.

In the scientific world there are perhaps no facts more clearly demonstrated than that the higher and complex *forms* of life have been gradually evolved through the ages from organisms so simple that they are composed of but one cell. In fact, our own bodies today arise from the single cell formed by the fusion of die masculine and feminine germ-cells of our parents. The science of biology shows not only each stage in the development of complex forms from the simple by the acquirement of new functions, but it can trace the beginning and progressive development of every organ and function, from the primitive differentiation of the protoplasm up to the fully developed nervous system and enormous brain of man; from the primitive "sensitive spot" to the fully developed eye; from the straight digestive tube to the complex digestive tract; from the straight pulsating blood vessel to the heart and complicated circulatory system, etc.

The science of embryology has proved that all forms evolve from a single cell. Furthermore, during its intra-uterine evolution each *form* of life passes successively through the stages of all the lesser forms below it in evolution. For instance, the human embryo like all mammals has its leaflike stage, its fish stage with gill-slits in the neck—one of which still persists as the eustachian tube connecting the ear with the mouth—its reptile stage, its mammal stage, etc.

In some stages the organs which are only vestiges in adult man are still prominent in the lower animals. For instance, at one stage of the human embryo the tail is longer than the leg, yet after birth the only trace of a tail is a rudimentary chain of bones at the lower end of the spine, the *coccyx*. There have been catalogued no less than 180 structures[1] that are but rudimentary or vestigial in man, altho these structures are fully developed and functioning in lower forms of animal life.

The science of comparative anatomy shows that there are no essential differences in the structure of man and many lower forms—the horse, dog, ostrich, whale, frog, etc.—only modifications of the same general plan. "The resemblance, after the first four weeks growth, between the embryo of a man and a dog is such that it is scarcely possible to distinguish them."[2] The embryo of the whale—which was once a land animal—is coated with hair, has rudimentary teeth and hind legs plainly apparent, and its skeleton still retains the rudimentary leg bones even tho their function has been discontinued.

Together with anthropology, the science of paleontology—the science of the fossil remains of animals—has collected a virtually complete series of fossil forms

---

[1] *The New Science and the Old Religion*, Jacobs, 245.
[2] Modern Science and Modern Thought, Laings, 171.

from the simplest trilobites and ammonites up to the most complex forms, the series of the changes in each form often being complete. The series showing the evolution of the horse from a five-toed creature scarcely larger than a rabbit up to the modern one-toed horse, for instance, is quite complete. The lowest and earliest strata of rocks show only the lowest types of shell forms, but the higher and more recent strata show, in precise succession, fishes, reptiles, birds and mammals.

Every general type-form in this imperishable and irrefutable record of the rocks is followed in precisely the same order by the development of the human embryo, showing that its form had been progressively developed through all those stages. Certain blanks in the geological record still occur, but certain fossil remains of man have been found which trace him back thru the close of the Pliocene period—a period which endured at least a quarter of a million years—into the still older Miocene period, which was certainly twice as long as the Pliocene. And in the Miocene strata many types of giant anthropoids have been found.

Yet the process of evolution is far from a mechanical one or we would not find primitive forms, from unicellular organisms up to man—such as the newly discovered tribes in New Guinea which are still in the Stone Age and without metal of any kind—still persisting. If it were merely a mechanical process all forms would have evolved practically together and we would now have only the highest types found today. Yet the Bushman and the Black Boy have made practically no advance above the most primitive stages, while many highly cultured races have flourished and disappeared. And highly civilized nations have suddenly been plunged backward into barbarism, not once in history, but many times, as the ruins of a score of empires mutely testify.

In fact nowhere do we find a constant, ever-flowing progress in every species. Nowhere is there evidence of one species uniformly—only approximately—shading off into the next higher, and so on up to man, as is claimed by the materialists as the absolute rule. The sudden breaks and gaps can only be explained as the result of a discriminating, super-physical Consciousness working out a predetermined plan.

"Certain well-marked forms of living beings have existed thru enormous epochs, surviving not only the changes of physical conditions (environment), but *persisting comparatively unaltered*, while other forms of life have appeared and disappeared. . . . and examples of them are abundant enough in both the animal and the vegetable worlds."[3]

Therefore, evolution is far from being the mere mechanical process which materialism would have us believe. "There is such a vast abyss between the anatomy and physiology of the larva and that of the perfect insect, that it is evidently impossible to find in natural selection the explanation of its ancestral

---

[3] *Proceedings of the Royal Institution*, Huxley, III, 151.

evolution."[4] There are many factors which science has not yet discovered or which it has refused to recognize.

"There is so much we do not yet understand. Will the day ever come when we can explain why the brain of man has made such great progress while that of the gorilla has fallen far behind? Can we explain why inherited ability falls to one family and not to another; or why, in the matter of cerebral endowment, one race of mankind has fared so much better than another? We have as yet no explanation to offer. . . . The final, decisive judgment on the theory of evolution may not be delivered in our time. Meanwhile, we think its most enlightened advocates would not claim more for it than that it is a *working hypothesis* which explains the known facts more satisfactorily than any other. . . . The conclusions may be right or they may be wrong, but they are not proved in the sense that a mathematical or chemical problem can be proved."[5]

Yet there is so much actual physical and logically irrefutable evidence as to the progressive evolution of *forms* that it cannot be ignored or denied. The important thing is that it all has to do with *forms* only, not with the causes or reasons for these forms, or the life-spirit and consciousness which animates them.

---

[4] *From the Unconscious to the Conscious*, Geley, 10.
[5] Presidential address of Sir Arthur Keith, hailed as "the most brilliant of anthropologists," before the *British Association for the Advancement of Science*, 1927.

"Nothing is really greater in the scope of the plan of an evolved universe than the growth of man from among the lowest forms of life to a being of intellect and soul, struggling to define his own relation to his Creator, aware of his obligations to his Creator and his fellowmen; developing a normal law of altruism, and a progress in self-restraint and duty to a Power higher than himself, which works for righteousness."[6]

---

[6] Ex-President William H. Taft, Address to *American Unitarian Association*, Oct. 13, 1927.

CHAPTER II

MATERIALISM

"Materialism in philosophy is the theory which regards all the facts of the universe as explainable in terms of matter and motion, and in particular explains all psychical processes by physical and chemical changes in the nervous system. . . . The business of the scientist is to explain everything by the physical causes which are comparatively well understood and to exclude the interference of spiritual causes." *Encyclopaedia Britannica*, xvii, 878.

"You cannot possibly synthesize Nature and leave out its most outstanding attributes. Nor can you get these potentialities out of Nature, no matter how far back you go. In other words, materialism, as commonly understood, is an altogether *absurd* and utterly *irrational* philosophy, and is indeed so regarded by most thoughtful men." Prof. Robert A. Milikan, *Collier's*, Oct 24, 1925, 5.

"By its whole biology the insect presents the symbol of what evolution really is, and it proves that *the essential cause* of evolution should be sought neither in the influence of the environment, nor in the reactions of organic matter to that environment; but in a dynamism *independent* of that organic matter *directing* it and *superior to it.*" *From the Unconscious to the Conscious*, Geley, 30.

Materialism is an evidence of intellectual vanity: the refusal of the intellect to admit that there is a Consciousness beyond its comprehension and aspects of Causation which it is unable to grasp.

In spite of the marvellous achievements of science

mentioned in the previous chapter, a close analysis will show that they have to do with physical things only: physical forms, conditions and appearances. They do not deal with ultimates, with either causation, origins or destinies. In fact, science deliberately shuts itself away from origins and destinies, saying that they belong in the domains of philosophy, metaphysics, theology and speculation. It therefore voluntarily limits itself to manifestations only; to phenomena; to things which can be seen, touched and handled or at least measured mechanically. It thus limits the scope of its investigations and its service to mankind quite as much as would one who was investigating the color of the spectrum if he declared that he would have nothing to do with the regions of the ultra-violet or the infra-red for the superficially plausible reason that they did not concern him because he could not see them! "Everything transcending the scheme of energetics is declared to be *superstition*. Everything transcending the limits of ordinary consciousness is declared to be *pathological*. A Chinese wall of 'positivistic' sciences and methods is built up around free investigation. Everything rising above this wall is condemned as *unscientific*."[1] In other words, in scientific materialism, "The business of the scientist is to explain everything by the physical causes," and refuse to discuss any other possibility.

Once given ultimates—life, energy, consciousness,

---

[1] *Tertium Organum*, Ouspensky, 344.

matter—materialism can furnish marvellous explanations of *processes*, but not of causes. It explains only the intricate mechanism by means of which those ultimates find expression in matter, for these are physical phenomena which come within the scope of its self-imposed limitations; phenomena which it can trace, weigh and measure. It can trace the transformation of energy from one form to another, but cannot explain its origin. It can analyze and catalog the chemical constituents of matter, but cannot explain its origin. It can trace the progressive evolution of the different *forms* thru which life manifests—from lowest to highest—but it cannot explain *why* life manifests thru any of them.[2] It can trace with microscopic accuracy the beautiful and complex mechanism by which life manifests in the body, its growth and repair, the end products of its activities, etc., but it cannot explain *life* itself. It can trace the avenues by which consciousness, operating thru the mind, affects certain brain centers to cause the movement of muscles and thereby give expression to the idea held in the mind, but it cannot explain mind or consciousness.

"They (scientists) seem to immerse us in a sort of self-acting mechanism, as if everything proceeded automatically without any conscious knowledge, ar-

---

[2] "I cannot explain why I am alive rather than dead. Physiologists can tell me a great deal about the mechanical and chemical processes of my body, but they cannot say why I am alive. But would it not be utterly absurd for me to deny I am alive?" Prof. Robt A. Mallikan, *Collier's*, Oct. 24, 1925, 5.

rangement, guidance or plan; as if it were a sort of haphazard universe. . . . as if the universe were a machine, a heartless, unmindful machine. Why? Because the business of science is to explore *mechanisms*, to detect *processes* by which all the functions of an organism are accomplished."[3]

With all its vaunted scientific attainments materialism cannot explain the origin of the universe or, even of the tiniest speck of protoplasm, much less can it explain life, consciousness, mind, love, altruism, self-sacrifice, duty, ideals, etc. Yet all these are just as *real* as wood, stone, iron or steel and are more powerful than any known material forces. For men give up their lives and suffer unspeakable tortures for an ideal, sacrifice their lives to save another from drowning or from a burning building, and often give up wealth, honor, position and family for a moral or spiritual principle.

Since materialism deals only with processes and materials, and explains neither life, death, existence, consciousness nor idealism, it fails us in every crisis of life, hence is not only an inadequate but a *false philosophy*. "The bankruptcy of materialism when it comes to organizing life on earth is now evident. . . . It becomes clearer that the changes in our outer life, when they come, will come *as a result of inner changes in man*."[4] As Prof. Millikan—the winner of the Nobel Prize for his revolutionary discoveries

---

[3] Sir Oliver Lodge, *New York Times*, March 25, 1928, 13.
[4] *Tertium Organum*, Ouspensky, 332.

in electricity—well says: "Materialism is an altogether absurd and entirely irrational philosophy, and is indeed so regarded by thoughtful men."

As a stimulus to physical research materialism has done wonders in analyzing materials and explaining processes, but as a philosophy it has been morally stultifying and spiritually a blight, almost a curse, in the lives of its followers. It has turned their attention from *causes* to their mere *effects*; from *origins* to *phenomena*. And, thru the promotion of agnosticism and atheism, it has stifled in many the innate instinct of the human Soul to believe in and seek to correlate with a Supreme Being, its Creator and Source.

But, thanks be, materialism as a philosophy is already dead and buried, altho some odors of its decaying corpse still linger in the back waters of the scientific world, in spite of the fact that the main current of scientific thought has long since swept on to new and higher conceptions.

The person who would appear scientific, yet still holds to the doctrine of materialism, simply displays his ignorance of the advances which have taken place in the scientific world, and is at least two decades behind the times. For materialism has been entirely abandoned and supplanted by dynamism as a theory of causation. In fact, matter, in the old sense of invisible physical particles, no longer exists, the atom having been shown to be but a phenomenal manifestation of two charges of electricity, a positive nucleus, the proton, surrounded by negative electrons.

As a distinguished Russian scientist, Prof. N. A. Oumoff, puts it: "The universe consists of positive and negative corpuscles, bound by electro-magnetic fields. Matter disappeared; its variety was replaced by a system of mutually related electric corpuscles, and instead of the accustomed material world one deeply different—the electro-magnetic world—is envisaging itself to us."[5] "But in such case," says Ouspensky, "the electrons must be regarded, not as electro-magnetic units, but as principles only, *i.e.*, as two opposite aspects, phases of the world, or in other words, as *metaphysical units*. The transition of physics into metaphysics is inevitable if the physicists desire to be simply logical." The theory as to matter has, therefore, disappeared, its place being taken by the theory of energy or force. Materialism, therefore, no longer has a leg to stand upon.

But no amount of stored energy can produce a living or even an organized form. The cause of forms is neither matter nor force; for back of any force, even life-force, must be the pattern which governs and delimits the form thru which the force manifests. The pattern cannot be produced without design. Design cannot be produced without the idea back of it. And ideas cannot be produced without intelligence. And intelligence cannot be manifested without mind. Causation, therefore, has been pushed back from matter to mind.

Some schools of thought, in their enthusiasm for

---

[5] *Tertium Organum*, Ouspensky, 117.

MATERIALISM

this great advance in scientific conception, go so far as to proclaim that "all is mind and mind is all," and that the brain is supreme. But modern advances in psychology, and especially in psychical research, show that we do not think with our brains, but with our *minds*, and that the mind can function entirely apart from the *brain*,[6] and survives it after its death and disintegration in the grave, as taught in every great religion and scientifically proved under test laboratory conditions by the mountains of evidence produced by scientific psychical research.[7] In fact, the brain is now known to be largely but the physical mechanism or switchboard by which sensory impulses from the outer physical world reach the mind, and by which ideas and thoughts in the mind move the appropriate muscles necessary for their expression in the physical world.

A little further consideration reveals the fallacy of the "mind is all" doctrine; for we only have to think a moment to realize that even mind is not the ultimate factor in causation. Back of mind must be the consciousness which merely uses the mind as a mechanism for the formulation and expression of its ideas into

---

[6] "In a native, aged forty-five years, suffering from cerebral contusion, the autopsy revealed a large abscess occupying nearly the whole left cerebral hemisphere. How did this man think? What organ was used for thought after the destruction of the region which, according to physiologists, is the seat of intelligence?" *From the Unconscious to the Conscious*, Geley, 81.

[7] For details see *Realms of the Living Dead*, Curtiss; *Photographing the Invisible*, Coates; *Phenomena of Materialisation*, Schrenck-Notzing, etc.

thoughts in the mental world, as the thought uses the brain as a mechanism of expression in the physical world. But back of consciousness there must still be That which is conscious, the Thinker. In its universal and cosmic aspect, it is indisputable that back of even Divine Mind there must be that self-existent Infinite Source of force, life and consciousness "whose center is nowhere and whose circumference is everywhere" which man calls God.

This Infinite Source is not a Being, yet from Its bosom spring all beings. It is not a Life, yet It is the Source of the One Life which animates all forms. It is not a Consciousness, yet It rules and governs and manifests through all focalized expressions of consciousness, from the highest Archangels, the mighty Heaven-born, whose consciousness is so vast, so all-pervading that we can but guess at its functioning, down through grade after grade of conscious living Beings to the consciousness of worlds, the consciousness of men, of animals and of Nature, down to the tiniest electron[8] that goes to make up the smallest and seemingly least important manifestation of all the vast solar systems of the universe. Each is a part of some aspect of God and a manifestation of His life, consciousness and power in its own plane and after its own kind.

---

[8] See *The Consciousness of the Atom*, Bailey.

CHAPTER III

THE LAW OF MANIFESTATION

"All things had their origin in Spirit-evolution [involution rather.—ED.], having begun above and proceeded downward, instead of the reverse, as taught in the Darwinian theory. In other words, there has been a gradual materialization of forms until a fixed ultimate of debasement is reached. This point is that at which the doctrine of modern evolution enters into the arena of speculative hypothesis." *Principles of Zoology*, Agassiz, 154.

"Evolution, in the latter [occultism], proceeds on quite different lines; the physical according to Esoteric teachings, evolving [or descending, etc.] from the spiritual, mental and psychic." *The Secret Doctrine*, Blavatsky, 238.

"It is the erroneous conclusions of physical science, which overlook God as the intelligence back of the evolutionary plan, that cause a great many people.... to disbelieve actual facts as well as this theory." *The Seventh Seal*, Agnes, 76.

In the previous chapter we have shown that neither matter nor force alone could produce an intricately organized form, even that of an amoeba without a pattern.[1] But where does the pattern come from? Throughout all ages the greatest philosophers man-

---

[1] "One cannot even conceive by what mysterious series of adaptations an insect, accustomed to larval life, underground, or in water, could succeed in gradually creating for itself wings for an aerial life, closed to it and doubtless unknown." *From the Unconscious to the Conscious*, Geley, 16.

kind has produced, as well as its greatest religious teachers, are in practical agreement that the patterns or Ideal Types of all forms and materials in Nature were outbreathed or projected from the mind of the Architect of the Universe at the beginning of each cycle of manifestation. As these Ideal Types descended through the various invisible worlds into physical manifestation they successively became mental and then ethereal or astral patterns before they became physically embodied or materialized. For the life-force which animates all forms which express it is a projective and impelling power which ever flows from within outward. In other words, the Law of Manifestation is that all manifestation proceeds from the invisible to the visible; from within outward; from the invisible pattern to its materialized expression in matter.

The proof of the correctness of this axiom is seen about us, on every hand, in Nature. In man we see his invisible ideas and desires moulding his thoughts, and his thoughts finding expression in and determining his words and acts, moulding his countenance and even modifying the contours of his head. Gladstone is said to have increased the size of his hat three times. Everywhere we see the inner pattern or idea moulding the outer manifestation; the invisible pattern gradually materialized by the synthesizing, cohesive and projective power of the life-force. Once the life-force pouring through the pattern is withdrawn, the physical form disintegrates into its component parts; for the cohesive, centripetal force which held them together is no longer present.

Why does a plant or animal stop growing in size when it has reached maturity? Why does an acorn grow into an oak tree and never into any other kind of a tree? Why does every seed in the vegetable world and every germ in the animal world reproduce its own kind? the tiniest pathogenic germ its own disease, and no other? Cut open an acorn and no tiny physical pattern of the future oak can be found, not even by the highest powered microscope. Yet it is evident that there must be a pattern, a particular pattern belonging to that species, and a specific pattern belonging to that individual tree. The fact that there is no pattern to be seen in the seed plainly shows that the seed is merely a focal point in matter thru which the life-force can flow into the earth and by its synthesizing power pick out from the earth the materials necessary to be built into the meshes of the invisible pattern to materialize that particular form. It selects not only the materials in general, but the particular chemicals needed to materialize that particular pattern and give it its specific properties, whether food, medicine, poison, etc. For this reason we see some plants or trees absorbing certain substances from the soil and other plants and trees growing side by side with them absorbing other substances from the same soil according to the nature of the pattern and properties to be materialized. The practical application of this Law of Materialization thru selective affinity is already utilized by the progressive farmer in his rotation of crops, or his soil would quickly become exhausted of certain materials by the repeated planting of one particular crop.

According to one Hebrew authority[2] this superphysical or mental creation of archetypal forms is expressly stated to be the basis of all manifestation. In the first verse of *Genesis*, instead of the conventional translation of, "In the beginning God created the heavens and the earth," the true meaning of the Hebrew words is, "Within His spiritual consciousness God chose and prepared for and decided to put the heavens and the earth into manifestation." The Hebrew phrase *Be-rashith* now translated "in the beginning" has no relation to time or the beginning of time, but means "the active power or principle within," hence mind or consciousness, while the word *Bara*, translated as "created," really means "preparation of movement toward form," hence preparation for manifestation in form.

But this materialization of the invisible pattern is not a mere mechanical process. Evolution clearly shows that forms are continually modified by some causative factor which tends toward a *predetermined* end, the perfection of the species.[3] Wherever we see

---

[2] *The Four-fold Process of God Creation*, Brown Landone, I, 5.
[3] "This it not the 'directive idea' of Claude Bernard, which is a kind of abstraction.... This is a concrete idea.... that of a directing and centralizing dynamism, dominating both intrinsic and extrinsic contingencies, the chemical reactions of the organic medium, and the influences of the external environment." *From the Unconscious to the Conscious*, Geley, 49.

THE LAW OF MANIFESTATION 37

a manifestation of life there we also see a manifestation of consciousness. In the kingdoms below man it is not human consciousness or self-consciousness, but nevertheless consciousness of a certain grade and upon its own plane. This is so well recognized that it has led to the formulation of the axiom, "No life without consciousness: no consciousness without life." Even the invisible, microscopic animalculae in a drop of stagnant water have been shown to possess all the fundamental characteristics which are accepted as tests of consciousness in the higher forms, namely, irritability, choice, volition, will, etc.[4]

An excellent example of the conscious activity of cells is seen in the uriniferous tubules of the kidney. Here one type of cells is followed by an entirely different type within the same tubule. The tall columnar cells select from the blood stream only the solid wastes that must be thrown out of the body, while the low, flat, epithelial cells lying next to them in the same tubule excrete only the liquid wastes. This is not a mere matter of osmosis or fluids soaking through an animal membrane until the specific gravity of the fluids on the two sides of the membrane is equalized; for if it were, all the fluids of the blood would soon be drained away like water through a sponge. That which appears as urine on the excreting side of the cells is not urine simply transferred from the blood to the excreting duct, for there is no urine in the blood, only the materials from which it can be

---

[4] For details see *The Psychic life of Micro-organisms*, Binet.

manufactured. Nor is this process a mere matter of chemotaxis, or mechanical chemical affinity. For in each case the two kinds of cells select from the common blood stream, which bathes them both, certain specific substances which they alone can handle. And these substances are not merely thrown out on the other side of the cell, but are transformed into quite different products. These new products are thrown out of the cell, not back again into the blood stream whence their materials were extracted, but are pushed out on the other side of the cell into the otherwise empty uriniferous ducts where there is neither chemical affinity (chemotaxis) nor negative osmotic pressure to attract them.

It is true that complicated chemical reactions do take place during this process, but they are not the result of mere proximity or propinquity of chemical substances. They are the result of: (a) the conscious selection by the cell of certain specific substances from the blood, (b) their transformation into quite other substances by the specific activity of the cell protoplasm, and (c) their intelligent and purposeful excretion into the one and only channel whereby they can be thrown out of the body, not only for the preservation of the health of the cells performing this service, but for the preservation of the health of the entire organism.

If the underlying normal chemistry of the body, *i.e.*, the alkalescence of all the body fluids (except four) and tissues, is upset by an excess of acid-forming foods,

THE LAW OF MANIFESTATION

deficient oxidation (exercise) and deficient excretion, the functioning of all the cells, tissues and organs is lessened and often perverted. The excess acid depletes the tissues of their calcium salts which make the nerves and tissues electrically conductive, and its place is taken by the electrically non-conductive magnesium salts. This calcium-depletion and magnesium-infiltration naturally loads up the cell protoplasm with inert material which obstructs the flow of the nerve currents—electric, thermic, mechanic, chemic and psychic (conscious and sub-conscious)—and the tissues thus deprived of their normal nerve stimulus are depleted in vitality and their functions both diminished and often perverted; for the acid excess diminishes the electrical conductivity, retards oxidation and the elimination of waste products and thus causes various retrograde changes—chronic inflammation, atrophy, hypertrophy, fibrosis and other degenerative changes—in the cells; among other things producing cytotoxines or cell poisons, which definitely interfere with the functions of the cells themselves and all the other functions and structures depending upon the products of the cell activities. This is especially true of the nervous system and the endocrine and other glands.

It is well known in progressive medical circles that acidosis, with its concomitant calcium-depletion and magnesium-infiltration,[5] is the great chemical factor

---

[5] For details see *The Chemic Problem in Nutrition*, Dr. John Aulde, Philadelphia, Pa.

underlying the body condition upon which the great majority of all diseases, both acute and chronic infections, neuritis, sciatica, arterio-sclerosis, arthritis, nephritis, etc.—ingraft themselves. For with the cells short-circuited from their normal stimuli, loaded with obstructive material and depleted in vitality they become an easy prey to all kinds of germs or other invasions.

But this chemical condition is not an argument against the consciousness and selective and purposive action of the cells. It is simply their reaction to the abnormal conditions of the body fluids – blood, lymph and chyle, whose integrity depends upon their alkalescence—upon which they must depend entirely for all their materials. And when their vitality is impaired by this calcium-depletion and magnesium-infiltration they cannot manifest the normal resistance to disease which we call natural immunity.

The above shows that while man's consciousness must be responsible for the treatment he gives to the body as a whole and for the accomplishment of the mission for which he incarnated in the flesh, every cell and every organ has a consciousness of its own, adapted to its work and competent to carry out its destined part in the Law of Manifestation, and intelligently adapt itself to the varying conditions imposed upon it.

Prof. Jagadis C. Bose, of the University of Calcutta, in his years of experimentation with plants has conclusively shown that even plants have not only a

THE LAW OF MANIFESTATION

quality of consciousness of their own, but also sensation; that they suffer from injury and respond to stimulus just as do animals. They can be poisoned by the same poisons that affect animals and can be revived by the same antidotes, etc.[6] Even fading, cut flowers in a vase can be revived and made to last longer by the addition of a simple stimulant such as aspirin.

We, therefore, in all cases see that back of the invisible pattern there is a life-force and a consciousness, an intelligence, an infinite power to move continually onward and upward, that is ever working toward the perfection of the form through which it finds expression. Man can work with, and to a degree guide, this lesser intelligence in various ways, such as cross-breeding, the prolonged use of the X-rays;[7] thru artificial fertilization—mechanical, chemical, electrical, etc.—which modify and often greatly accelerate the perfection of the form, just as an undeveloped man can be improved and assisted toward perfection thru education. But in both cases the control of the process is only within certain well recognized limits. It has been shown that "no amount of uplift, education or opportunity can develop a new race of men of initiative, creative intelligence, resourcefulness and self-command out of the stupid and ineffective who have to be told what to do and how to do it. This is the eugenic and biological

---

[6] *Life and Work of Sir Jagadis C. Bose*, 147.
[7] See *Experiments of Dr. H. J. Muller*, University of Texas, also of Dr. Wm. H. Dieffenbach, New York Homeopathic Medical College.

contention against which environmentalists of the sentimental school vainly declaim. The facts are against them."[8]

This continual modification of the form toward perfection, and from lower and simpler forms to higher and more complex forms, science rightly calls evolution, for it is an evoluting or unfolding outwardly of *that which has already been involved* (involution) within the invisible pattern.[9] The embryo, for instance, is a huge congeries of intricately interdependent tissues, organs and functions. Biologists are only beginning to ask how the differing activities and needs of these various tissues and organs are regulated, their freedom of function protected and their maneuvers timed and synchronized in perfect harmony. All work together for the best good, not only of each cell, tissue and organ, but for the best good of that larger unit of which they are but parts, the growing organism itself, of whose appearance, consciousness and function as a whole the cells and organs can have no possible conception or even awareness. Just as the vast majority of persons have no conception of the Universal or Over-Soul of humanity in Whose body of

---

[8] *The Builders of America*, Huntington and Whitney.

[9] "How could the reptilian ancestor of the bird adapt itself to surroundings which were not its own and could only become its own *after* it had passed from the reptilian to the bird form? Before possessing usable (not embryonic) wings it could not have an aerial life to which to adapt itself. . . . A reptile with embryonic wings, or wings indicated at the beginning of their development, has never been found." *From the Unconscious to the Conscious*, Geley, 15, 25.

manifestation they are but individualized cells, and Whose perfect manifestation can never be perfected until all its constituent cells (individualized Souls) reach their individual perfection.

No answer has ever been found to this problem and none will ever be found that does not postulate the intelligence of a directing Mind, a discriminating super-physical Consciousness, back of the invisible pattern which both determines and controls the organism.

Just now science is worshipping energy or the force of the atom, the electron, etc., and endeavoring to ascribe all power to it, just as it formerly worshipped matter and ascribed all causation to it. But just as it found in matter no explanation of causation, neither will it find such an explanation in force; for neither matter nor undirected force—nor both combined—can create form without a pattern, nor a pattern without consciousness.

The materialists still refuse to recognize consciousness as a factor in the process of evolution because their philosophy of life is too narrow to account for its presence. Consequently they endeavor to explain its cause by wholly mechanical factors:[10] the elder Darwin by the effect of environment; Charles Darwin by sexual selection; Lamarck by use and disuse; De Vries by mutation; Nageli by specific ideo-plasm, and others by heredity, etc., all holding that in some *admittedly unknown* way it must result from the mechanical reaction of the organism to the various fac-

---

[10] *The Mechanistic Conception of Life*, Loeb.

tors in its life and environment. And the very fact that there are so many theories as to causation shows that no one and no combination of them is wholly satisfactory even to the materialists themselves.

Since the progressive evolution of life-forms in Nature is according to a predetermined design, or the unfoldment and outward manifestation of that which has been involved and is already inherent within, it cannot be satisfactorily accounted for or understood except as the gradual manifestation in matter of Ideal Types or Archetypes, created in the higher worlds by the various angelic Creative Hierarchies and consciously manifested by the various grades of Intelligences who are their agents. "The cause of the underlying physiological variation of the species—one to which all other laws are subordinate and secondary—is a sub-conscious intelligence pervading matter, ultimately traceable to a reflection of the Divine and Dhyan-Choanic Wisdom."[11]

The immediate pre-physical patterns are progressively modified by the Creative Hierarchies according to the stage of evolution, the varying outer conditions, etc., so there may seem to be mistakes made, but they are all part of the various stages of adaptation to conditions, yet in a general progression toward the ultimate manifestation of the ideal.[12] "The evolution

---
[11] *The Secret Doctrine*, Blavatsky, II, 685.
[12] "Humanity as a whole is not so isolated as it had thought. It is but a temporarily materialized portion of a great spiritual world, wherein are powers and affections and intelligences innumerable, intelligences outside of the scope of our senses, but watchful and helpful to the utmost of their permitted power." Sir Oliver Lodge, *New York Times*, March 25, 1928, 13.

of the *external* form, or body, around the astral, is produced by the terrestrial forces, just as in the case of the lower kingdom; but the evolution of the *Internal* or real *Man* is purely spiritual."[13]

We think this brief outline of the Law of Manifestation is sufficient to show that because science ignores the essential factors of causation in evolution, *i.e.*, intelligence, plan and purpose, its entire viewpoint is limited and its basic theories as to *origins* and *causes* are, therefore, necessarily inadequate, and hence must ultimately be revised. Instead of evolution being the *mechanical reaction* of the organism to its environment, it is due to the *conscious adaptation* of the organism to its environment. It is the guidance of Intelligence and Purpose working toward the ever more perfect manifestation of the Ideal Type for each species.

Since the human body belongs to the animal kingdom, it too has reached its present state of perfection by such conscious adaptation and evolution from the lower forms thru the progressive manifestation of its invisible Archetype or pattern which contains all that man will eventually manifest as he evolves Godward out of the human kingdom into the super-human. But how are we to reconcile these conclusively demonstrated biological facts with the theological doctrine of creation? That is the problem of this volume.

---

[13] *The Secret Doctrine*, Blavatsky, I, 198

CHAPTER IV

CREATION

> "And God said, Let us make man in our image, after our likeness. . . . So God created man in his own image, in the image of God created he him; male and female created he them." *Genesis*, I, 26-7.

> "There is an ever-increasing number of persons who refuse to accept former religious teachings unless they are given, not merely dogma and creed, but a rational and scientific explanation of the basis of their claims." *The Message of Aquaria*, Curtiss, 375.

Creations cannot be the result of mere mechanical mixtures or chemical activities. The intricate organization of all forms, from amoeba to man, and the perfect synchronizing of all their varied functions, is in itself irrefutable evidence of both *plan* and *purposive organization* toward a *predetermined end*. All of this is necessarily the result of organized and purposive consciousness controlling powers and forces necessary for its manifestation.

Both the creation of Ideal Types and their evolution in matter, or their gradual unfoldment after their descent from the subjective worlds into materialization on Earth, seem to mankind a tremendously, almost infinitely, slow process. Geology tells us that after the materialization of the Earth began, "1,000 million years is a *moderate minimum*" for the time required to lay down the sedimentary layers of the Earth's crust, from the earliest Palaeozoic and Cambrian rocks to the comparatively recent glacial clays and gravels and the present day alluvium and peat deposits.

Professor John Walter Gregory, of Glasgow, has estimated the age of the Earth at 8,000 million years. Professor Arthur Eddington, of Cambridge, arrived at the same figure from astronomical data. Lord Rayleigh arrived at the same figure from still other data. And Prof. A. W. Bickerton of London, and Dr. James Hopwood Jeans, Secretary of the Royal Astronomical Society of London, consider the Earth much older.

If we could stratify and examine the sea in the same way we would find that it also had passed through corresponding changes—from the ages in which it was largely composed of carbonic acid down to the present day salty sea water—and within its depths we would find many prehistoric forms of life. In fact, the more we search the earth and the sea, and the more we study the awesome changes—the mighty upheavals, subsidences and disappearances—which are still taking place today, the more convincing the evidence and the deeper becomes the conviction that the stupendous processes of creation and evolution are not yet completed; indeed, are still continuing, both in the body of the planet and in the body of man and the lower kingdoms.

Since we have shown that the Law of Manifestation is the process whereby the invisible pattern of every form—whether in Nature or man-made—is gradually materialized into its physical expression, and since we see proofs everywhere around us of this conception being correct, how can we reconcile this self-evident law with the traditional teaching of the *Bible* as to the origin of man? It is very simple, for the *Bible* teaches *exactly the same law*, and in almost the same words.

In the second chapter of *Genesis* (4-5) we read: "These are the generations of the heavens and of the earth when they were created, in the day that the Lord God made the earth and the heavens, and every plant of the field *before it was in the earth*, and every herb of the field *before it grew*." Here we have the doctrine of the formation of Ideal Types or pre-physical patterns precisely stated. At the early stage of manifestation indicated in the first, and part of the second, chapter of *Genesis* all forms were still subjective, ethereal and pre-physical, not having as yet descended into physical manifestation.

If there is a fundamental law in Nature whereby *everything* manifesting on Earth is first conceived in the mind of its creator and imaged forth in the substance of the invisible super-physical worlds before it descends into physical materialization or grows on Earth, then that law must apply to man as well. But lest someone objects to our use of the word *everything*, let us point out that this same Law of Manifestation applies to man's creations as well as to God's.

CREATION

If a building, automobile or other invention is to be constructed it must first be conceived in the mind of its creator and an exact mental pattern formed. This pattern is then outpictured as a drawing, and finally the masons, carpenters and other artizans build into that pattern the physical materials until the completed building or machine is but a materialization of its invisible mental pattern. And so with all man's creations. Even his words and acts are but physical expressions of his thoughts and desires. They are all outward expressions of invisible patterns which in their turn are but concrete mental forms thru which their ideas find expression.

In the first chapter of *Genesis* (26-27) we read: "And God said, Let us make man in our image, after our likeness. . . . So God *created* man in his image, in the image of God created he him: male and female created he them."

Here we have the statement that is the backbone of the Fundamentalists' claims; and they are quite right to cling to it as correct. But is this statement made concerning the physical body of man? Is it created in the Image of God? No thinking person can be so foolish as to maintain that it is our imperfect and *still evolving* physical bodies that were created in the Image of God! Certainly not! This refers to the formulation of the Ideal Type of man in the mind of God. The formation of the physical body is not referred to until the second chapter and is an entirely different thing. His body is but the outer building which ultimately results from the materialization of the inner idea, the Ideal Type, plan or pattern. The Adam of the first chapter is an entirely different being from the Adam of the second chapter. This first Adam is the Ideal or Spiritual Man, the Inner or Higher Self, the Divine Androgyne. This is a purely spiritual being and usually the one generally, altho loosely, referred to as the Soul of man.

This Spiritual Man has naught to do as yet with physical manifestation or with matter; in fact, no spiritual being, force or consciousness, nor even a mental or thought-form or thought-force, can manifest in any world except thru a suitable form, body or mechanism composed of the substance of the world in which it is to manifest: of spiritual substance in the spiritual world, mental substance in the mental world, astral substance in the astral world and physical substance in the physical world. It is only this Spiritual Man, created in the spiritual world, that is truly the Son of God, since he is created in His image and after His likeness; an individualized emanation of His consciousness and substance: the very Image of God.

According to one Hebrew scholar[1] who has devoted many years' study to the root meanings of the Hebrew words used in *Genesis*, the word Adam is an Egyptian mystery-word brought into the Hebrew language by Moses, who was learned in all the mysteries of the Egyptian priests. "Primarily the word Adam is composed of three roots: the first means *power within*, the second *similarity*, and the third *tendency to assimilate*. Therefore, this giving of activity to man by God includes: (1) God's giving to Adam a secret power *within*, *similar* to the power of God; (2) God's capacity of being assimilated *by Adam*; and (3) Adam's capacity to assimilate actively in the *similarity* of God. . . . Thus man has, first, absolute rule and dominion in *assimilating* God in the likeness of God, *manifesting* as God. Second, man has absolute rule and dominion over all processes of creation, each producing its own kind in his Soul in accord with the creative impulse— from the Spiritual Man—existing within itself. Third, man has complete and absolute power in using the activity given him, and this activity is like unto the actions of God. Fourth, man is in complete control and dominion of the growth of Soul manifestation. . . . The Samaritan Version, the oldest and most reliable, uses a synonym after the word Adam. This synonym means 'universal' or 'general'. Consequently, Adam is the *Universal Man*, the *Infinite Man*. So far as the English is concerned, the best translation of Adam is mankind."[1]

This Spiritual Man, therefore, has inherently within him, not only the potencies, but the actual emanations of all the God-powers and potencies—the God-Consciousness, the God-wisdom, the God-love, the God-compassion, and the God-power of creativeness— is in very truth "one with the Father, full of grace and

---

[1] *Seven El Ohim Cycles of Manifestation*, Brown Landone, VII, 1-4.

truth." He is as inseparable from the Father or Universal Spirit as the sunbeam is from the Sun. The sunbeam is not the Sun but it is of the Sun, an emanation containing all the potencies and powers of the Sun.

This Spiritual Man or Higher Self is the animating Spirit or personal aspect of God within each human being. It is both the personal Father-in-heaven and also the Christ within of each individual, both the Sun in the heavens and the sunbeam imprisoned within the fruit.[2] It may be compared to a virgin who has all the possibilities of love, tenderness, creativeness and fruitfulness within her, but as yet unmanifested materially.

While this Spiritual Man is all-knowing, all-loving, all-powerful and perfect while dwelling with the Father in the spiritual world, he has not fulfilled his destiny until he has manifested all his God-powers in *all* the worlds of manifestation, even the lowest and densest—this physical world. But to do this he must have a vehicle for such manifestation, a body composed of the substance of the world in which he is to manifest. How does he get such a body? This is explained in the second chapter of *Genesis*, 7. "And the Lord God *formed* man of the dust of the ground, and breathed into his nostrils the breath of life; and man became a living soul."

Apparently the first and second chapters are in flat contradiction. The first represents the teachings of the Ephraimite or Elohist School of writers, often

---
[2] *The Key to the Universe*, Curtis, 260-3.

called the Late Priestly Narrative, written between 450 and 400 B.C. The second chapter represents the Judean or Yahwist (Jehovistic) School, often called the Early Judean Prophetic. This second narrative was written *several hundred years earlier* (about 825 B.C.) than the first and certainly over three thousand years *after* the events were *supposed* to have taken place!

In the first chapter the lower kingdoms are represented as being created first and in their proper evolutionary order, and man is created last. In the second chapter the order is reversed and man is represented as being created first and then the lower kingdoms. In the first chapter man is represented as created dual, "male and female created He them," while in the second chapter Adam alone is formed and later on Eve.

This is a statement whose misunderstanding has caused a great deal of controversy. Apparently this is in flat contradiction to the statement made in the first chapter. The first states that man was created a *spiritual* being in the image and likeness of God, while the second states that he was composed of *matter*, formed of the dust of the ground. Can both these contradictory statements be true? If not which are we to believe? We are to believe both, for both are true, but they refer to entirely different things; the first to the Real or Spiritual Man and the second to the physical man or *body* which is absolutely essential for the Spirit's manifestation in material conditions.

CHAPTER V

CREATION (*CONCLUDED*)

> "I find then a law, that, when I would do good, evil is present with me. For I delight in the law of God *after the inward man*: but I see *another law* in my members, warring against the law of my mind, and bringing me into captivity to the law of sin which is in my members. O wretched man that I am! who shall deliver me from the body of this death?" Romans, VII, 21-24.

> "We may thus conceive of a dynamic and psychological complex *above the material* and organic complex, organizing and centralizing it. . . . the *real Self*, one and indivisible." *From the Unconscious to the Conscious*, Geley, 38.

In considering these two verses in *Genesis*, referred to in the previous chapter, it should be noted that there is a vast difference in the two processes described in the two chapters. The word translated as "created" in the first chapter is the Hebrew word *Bara* whose root meaning is found in many ancient languages—Chaldaic, Samaritan, Arabic, etc.—all of which indicate "that the basic root *is a choice* or an *intention* or *preparation of movement toward form*."[1] In this connection it indicates that God intended and prepared in thought for a formation, or made choice of an individualized aspect of Himself for expression in those worlds of manifestation which He had just

---
[1] *Seven El Ohim Cycles of Manifestation*, Landone, VI, i.

CREATION

projected from His Divine Consciousness into form.[2]

The word in the second chapter translated as "formed" is the Hebrew word *Yatsar* which means "formative imagination." This plainly indicates that the man of the second chapter was the physical body or animal man who was not *created* or projected spiritually in the image and likeness of God but was fashioned by the activity of a creatively formed and projected thought-form or invisible pattern which animated the dust of the ground, just as every beast of the field and every fowl of the air was "formed" out of the dust of the ground.[3] Here is the solution of the whole conflict between the Fundamentalists and the scientists; for this second man is the *animal form* which science has conclusively shown was slowly evolved from lower forms thru untold ages, while the first man is the Spiritual Man or Image of God which was not evolved, but *created* by the conscious intention of the Godhead to manifest Himself in form.[4]

As explained elsewhere: This, of course, does not mean that God gathered up a handful of dust and fashioned man out of it, but it does mean, that the Divine Ideation, through the *creative power* of the Cosmic Consciousness and the *manifesting power* of the One Life, first conceived the idea and then projected it into objective manifestation: first the idea

---

[2] "We may understand that the birth and evolution of a world is a vast materialization of the universal dynamo-psychism."—*From the Unconscious to the Consious*, Geley, 284.
[3] *Genesis*, II, 19.
[4] *The Four-fold Process of God Creation*, Landone, I, 5.

of the Earth and all things pertaining to it, and finally man himself, all fashioned out of the same fundamental and undifferentiated Cosmic Substance and then clothed in a body of flesh composed of earthly substances.[5]

But until this animal form had reached a certain degree of perfection it was but a human animal and *not man* as we know him today. When the proper stage of evolution had been reached, something most extraordinary took place: an addition was made which raised this animal form out of the fourth kingdom of Nature (the animal) into the fifth kingdom (the human) and made that ape-like animal form more than animal. This extraordinary advance took place when God "breathed into his nostrils the breath of life." What was the result? This human animal then "became a living soul." Manifestly the "breath of life" does not refer to oxygen or the ordinary air, for all animal forms breathed that in their nostrils and had ordinary physical life. What was breathed in was the "pneuma" or the Spirit, and only because man then possessed a Spirit did he become a living Soul.

A body of flesh is essential, for without it the Soul cannot manifest on Earth, but it must be a body so evolved that it was capable, physically, mentally and spiritually, of ultimately expressing the life and consciousness of the Supreme Intelligence as the individualized consciousness of the incarnating Soul. Yet after the incarnation of the Soul the organism must

---

[5] *The Message of Aquaria*, Curtiss, 126.

be trained to co-operate with the indwelling Soul that its infinite powers may ultimately be manifested. In other words, only when, through the slow process of evolution from lower forms, a physical body had been evolved which contained the necessary functions, faculties, organs, centers and powers which were essential for the Soul's complete manifestation on Earth did the Spiritual Man descend and incarnate in that animal form. And because of his presence therein he gave it a living Soul.

Thus does the mystic disarm the materialist by gladly accepting all the *proved facts* of science, if not their materialistic and hence limited interpretation, and show how they all fit into their proper place in the divine Plan of Manifestation, once we understand the fundamentals of the Cosmic Philosophy which explains that great Plan.

As we have said elsewhere: Spiritual Beings. . . . consciously descended to Earth and breathed into the human-animal forms "the breath of life," as recorded in *Genesis*. That which is called the breath was something with which animal man was only then endowed—a power and capacity added to the mere animal consciousness which he possessed before; for it was the breath of Divine Life, a human Soul, a spiritual overshadowing.[6]

Realize that life here in the physical world is not something separate from Life in the higher realms, but is simply a continuation of that Life downward into

---

[6] *The Voice of Isis*, Curtiss, 233.

a denser medium of expression. We also find that the body is not a mere mechanism, but a living and highly intelligent animal with the functions, desires, appetites and habits of any animal. Hence it needs training and control, just as does any other high-bred animal, if it is to become a willing, obedient and efficient servant of its lord and master,[7] the indwelling Spiritual Man.

With the incarnation of the Spiritual Man in the animal body the great conflict of the two natures for control begins, for the animal nature naturally strives to gratify its desires, while the Spiritual Man strives to guide it toward constructive ends in accordance with Divine Law. As we have already said: This animal body of yours has certain desires and tendencies which are perfectly natural to it just as they are to any animal, but since you, the Immortal Self, are dwelling in it, you, the Immortal Self, must control the animal with its desires and tendencies and make it subservient to the Law of Being. The lower animals—having no individualized spark of the Divine dwelling in them.... follow their natural tendencies, when not perverted by contact with man, and these tendencies, not being perverted, are necessarily right and proper, but man, having a higher guidance than instinct, must control the animal tendencies instead of being controlled by them.[8] In fact; it is one of the great aims of human manifestation for the Soul to

---
[7] *The Message of Aquaria*, Curtiss, 175.
[8] *The Voice of Isis*, Curtiss, 215-16.

CREATION

perfect a body so spiritualized and trained that it will do the will of the Father on Earth, even as it is done in Heaven by the Soul.

As clearly explained by Jesus in speaking of the Spiritual Man within: "I came down from heaven, not to do mine own will, but the will of Him that sent me. And this is the Father's will which hath sent me, that of all [the powers and potencies] which he hath given me I should lose nothing, but should raise it up again at the last day."[9]

We thus see why it is, that while the Real Man is an immortal Spiritual Being, created perfect in the heavenly worlds, when he is limited in his expression on Earth, not only by a material body but one which is unfinished and still evolving, only thru eons of time and manifesting thru such a body during myriads of incarnations can he gain the experience in material embodiment necessary to dominate completely and control the animal organism and make it truly express the Divine Consciousness of his Real Self. It is because the animal body has all the appetites, desires and inherent selfishness of any animal and because these continually struggle for unrestricted indulgence, when unhampered by the guidance of the Divine Consciousness, that St. Paul said: "For we know that the law is spiritual: but I [the animal man] am carnal. . . . For I know that in me (that is, in my flesh) dwelleth no good thing: for to will is present with me; but how to perform that which is

---

[9] *St. John*, VI, 38-9.

good I find not. For the good that I would I do not: but the evil which I would not, that I do. Now if I do that I would not, it is no more I that do it, but sin [or animal desires] that dwelleth in me. I find then a law, that, when I would do good, evil is present with me. For I delight in the law of God *after the inward man*: but I see another law in my members, warring against the law of my mind, and bringing me into captivity to the law of sin which is in my members."[10] St. Paul here clearly distinguishes between the guidance of the Spiritual Man and the desires of the animal man. Yet "the flesh is a thing of habit; it—through the subconscious mind—will repeat mechanically a good impulse as well as a bad one. It is not the flesh which is always the tempter; in nine cases out of ten it is the Lower Manas—or human mind—which by its (creative) images, leads the flesh into temptation. . . . The higher (or spiritual) Mind directs the Will: the lower turns it into selfish Desire."[11]

We therefore see that the "fall of man," which the unillumined speculations of theologians have decided was due to the sin of our first parents, was not due to sin at all, but was the fall of the Spiritual Man into material embodiment as the *natural and inevitable* result of the Law of Manifestation. The "fall" was indeed great: the descent of a celestial being into mortality; from the pure, beatific state of being and

---

[10] *Romans*, VII, 14-23.
[11] *The Secret Doctrine*, Blavatsky, III, 539.

consciousness of the Spiritual World, down into a dense and unresponsive animal body which was dominated by its will to live and propagate its species. This descent into Earth conditions was also a great sacrifice.

As we have already pointed out: The Law of Sacrifice[12] must be a principle of divine manifestation. As the Creative Ray is sent forth into manifestation from the Divine, something of its divinity, purity and power is of necessity sacrificed by the limitations of every successive form through which it expresses, from the ideal thought-forms in the Universal Mind down through their manifestation in ethereal substance, until they reach their densest expression in physical matter. Each step of the descent is a sacrifice of a higher state and degree of consciousness that a lower form may exist. . . . It was brought about by the same great Principle of Divine Love and Wisdom, the Voice of the Deity sent forth, the Word that was spoken and sent forth thru all spheres in which the Spiritual Monad had to manifest to complete his Cycle of Necessity,[13] or cycle of projection, manifestation and indrawing. This "fall" was therefore not a "sin," nor due to the use of the sex functions, for the fall began in the higher realms *long before those functions were manifested* physically in the separated sexes. While the descent of the Soul into material

---

[12] See "The Law of Sacrifice," *The Message of Aquaria*, Curtiss, 254-76.
[13] See "The Cycle of Necessity" in *The Voice of Isis*, Curtiss, 284-94.

embodiment was a "fall," it was not a "fall" for man to use faculties, functions and "as gods" and "as one of us," the Elohim. For these were the very means given him wherewith to achieve his destiny; to rise to Godhood.

With this understanding of the real nature of the "fall" of man, it will be seen that the monstrous doctrine of "original sin" was but a mistaken medieval deduction from a false premise due to the failure of the early Church Fathers and Councils to distinguish between the Adam of the first chapter and the Adam of the second chapter: the same failure that is being made by both parties to the controversy today.

The Calvinistic doctrine of original sin holds that: "Adam in his fall involved the whole human race descended from him. Hence depravity and corruption, diffused thru all parts of the Soul, attached to all men. . . . These are held vitiated in all parts of their nature, and on account of such corruption deservedly condemned of God. . . . Adam's sin is, as a penalty, transmitted to all his descendants, both as guilt and as weakness. . . . even infants are involved in Adam's condemnation."[14]

We must remember that this terrible and debasing doctrine is not a teaching inspired by God, nor is it contained in the *Bible* story, but is the *mere opinion of one man* living in an age of persecution and bigotry, and who very evidently did not have the enlightenment of direct spiritual inspiration or of a Cosmic

---

[14] *Encyclopedia Britannica*, V, 26; XXV, 135.

CREATION

Philosophy to guide his speculations. But it is high time we use a little common sense, not to say spiritual intuition, and stop blindly following after such a debasing idea, just as we have stopped following the far more plausible doctrine of "the evil eye." As we have said elsewhere: The exaltation of the intellect and *man's refusal to follow his Inner Guidance*, together with his effort to subserve the spiritual forces within to bring temporal domination and the gratification of the lower senses, passions and desires was the "original sin" of the early Races, not the use of the creative powers themselves. This is clearly shown by the fact that the creative powers were given to man by his Maker and he was told to use them,[15] long before he misused these powers and was cast out of the Garden of Eden.

It should be noticed here that there is no time limit placed on the process of the formation of the animal body, and it may well have required the millions of years which both science and cosmic philosophy claim for it. The statement that Adam was formed out of the *dust* of the ground gives a hint as to the time that must have elapsed before there was any dust. For it must have taken many ages before the land was upheaved above the waters, and still other ages for the rocks thus upheaved to disintegrate through erosion and become dust.

We now understand that the so-called "days" of creation were not days of twenty-four hours, but vast

---

[15] *The Message of Aquaria*, Curtiss, 396.

geological ages. As a matter of fact, geology has proved that the Earth was created in six such "days" or ages, for the structure of the planet itself shows just six such vast eras, *i.e.,* the *Pre-zoic* or the stage from gaseous fire-mist to dense physical matter, the *Archeozoic*, *Proterozoic*, *Palaeozoic*, *Mesozoic*, and the *Cenozoic* or present age, which is still evolving and revealing its wonders. While the *Bible* was never intended to be a scientific or accurately historical treatise, nevertheless it is sufficiently accurate to have modern scientific research confirm its general order of creation.

For instance, *Genesis* tells us that there was light several "days" (eons) before the Sun, Moon and stars were created. Only a few years ago this statement was laughed at in scientific circles, but we now know that the nebula from which our solar system—one of the smallest—was condensed shone as brilliantly by its own inherent light as those we now observe in die heavens undergoing the same process, according to the universal Law of Manifestation.

Again science tells us that life began under water in the primordial ooze, and that as dry land arose out of the waters the higher forms of life gradually appeared. The *Bible* gives us precisely the same order of events, the Earth being without form (land) and covered with the waters of the deep. As the light appeared those germs of life in the waters were activated and began the unfoldment of their inner patterns in accordance with the Law of Manifestation. As the land appeared

CREATION 65

the higher forms progressively appeared one after the other, first vegetation—grass, herbs, trees, etc.—then "moving creatures" (reptiles) fowls, mammals and lastly man, in almost the exact order of evolution found by science recorded in the rock strata of the Earth.

Again we see that when we gain understanding of both evolution and what the *Bible* says about it, we find *there is no conflict between science and the Bible* in this respect. As one famous scientific authority says: "The spiritually inspiring thing which the biologists have shown us is that all life has progressed from the lowest toward the highest. If one does not believe that life has been a progressive development, step by step, *under the guidance of a co-ordinating principle*, then he has a very poor idea of divinity. For if life has progressed from small beginnings up to man in, say, ten million years, where will it be ten million years from now? Man is revealed by science as a being who is constantly progressing from glory to glory, changing more and more toward the *spiritual image* of his Creator."[16]

---

[16] Prof. Michael Pupin of Colombia University, *American Magazine*, September, 1927.

CHAPTER VI

MANIFESTING THE CREATION

"Long under the domination of materialism and positive thinking, forgetting and perverting religious ideas, men thought that it was possible to live by the merely logical mind alone. But, now, little by little, it is becoming quite evident to those who have eyes, that merely by the exercise of logical reason men will not be able to organize their life on earth." *Tertium Organum*, Ouspensky, 335.

"The totality of evolution, like its details, reveals an *obvious purpose* which neither selection nor adaptation nor any of the classical factors can sufficiently explain. . . . By reason of the ideal adaptation which it implies, this acquired purpose alone allows of the complete operation of the classical factors—natural selection, influence of the environment, sexual selection, segregation, migration, etc." *From the Unconscious to the Conscious*, Geley, 279.

"For the law of the Spirit of Life. . . . hath made me free from the law of sin and death. . . . That the righteousness of the law might be fulfilled in us, who walk not after the flesh, but after the Spirit." *Romans*, VIII, 2, 4.

Since man is a "microcosm of the macrocosm" or an epitome of the universe, to utilize the ideas set forth in the previous chapters let us here review them briefly as they apply to our own personal life and unfoldment.

At first thought many students find it hard to realize that man's body is as unfinished and unperfected an evolutionary product as is his personality and its human mind. Yet if we stop to think clearly we will readily recognize that this is so; for we know that the inner Spiritual Body—represented in the biblical allegory by the first Adam—was created as a perfect Pattern or Ideal Type. Gradually this Ideal Type descended into matter through *involution*, and then began the slow process of manifesting its perfection through *evolution*. Thus evolution progresses according to the degree in which the subtle creative forces of the invisible pattern are able to manipulate and make dense physical matter respond, altho for ages it responded only in a crude, rough general way to that pattern. And even this slow process of overcoming the inertia of matter and making it more responsive to the inner vibrations has been further retarded by man's disobedience, wrong thinking and mistaken religious teaching.

Ultimately we must manifest the Image of God in which the Real or Spiritual Self is created. But how few of even those who seek to live close to the Divine Ideal, at least in thought, find it possible at this stage of our evolution to manifest that Image as perfect harmony of mind and body, perfect functioning and health of every organ and part! For not only do we find functional disorders, due to our ignorance or carelessness of the laws of health,—diet, exercise, etc.—and to infections, etc., but we also have to meet the hereditary defects of the family in which we have incarnated, as well as the karmic conditions which we bring over from past lives, all of which will be spared us when those conditions have been worked out and our bodies have been fully evolved and perfected.

Today, the more we advance the more sensitive we become to all these personal conditions and also to world conditions. And the faster we work out our personal Karma the more we are able to help redeem the world Karma which we share with the rest of mankind. This is one of the mystical meanings of the crucifixion. For the more we become one with the Christ, the more Christ-force we have with which to conquer these conditions and thus help lift the burdens of humanity and say: "Father, forgive them; for they know not what they do."

At present our Spiritual Body is much like a small sapling which is destined to become a great tree but which has been planted in the crude soil of an animal body where it is subjected to tempestuous gusts of passion, gnawing desires and scorching emotions. It, therefore, still needs the oversight and guiding care of the great Gardener upon whom it must depend during its early stages of growth ere it can become the giant tree whose strength, beauty and fruitfulness can scarcely be imagined from the appearance of the mere sapling. For the most powerful microscope can discover no trace of a pattern of the future tree in the seed, nor does the outer appearance of the sapling give any indication of what its blossom and fruit will be. The very appearance of these are miracles in themselves; yet the pattern or Ideal Type of the tree and its fruit already exists in the invisible worlds. And as the pattern is materialized thru the Law of Growth it will gradually unfold and determine the size and type of tree and the kind of flower and fruit.

As we have already explained, the body of man is "of the earth earthy" just as is the seed of the tree. Yet like the seed it has within it an invisible ethereal pattern[1] which endeavors to reflect, as far as it has evolved, the perfection of its Ideal Type, or the Spiritual Body of the Inner Man or Real Self. Let us think then of our Real Self not merely as a vague, shadowy, formless Divine Essence, but as possessing a perfected and glorious Spiritual Body, the Ideal Type which shall ultimately manifest on Earth, perfect in every part, organ and function, and filled with radiant vitality, health and joy of living. But if our Real Self is clothed in such perfection that no inharmony, deformity, disease, sin, sickness or death can abide in it, why is it that our physical body is so incomplete, imperfect, unresponsive to the Real Self and prone to all the ailments to which the flesh is heir?

The first explanation is that the physical body is still evolving and has not yet reached a point where the Real Self can shine through or manifest, except to a very limited degree. Just as the life-cycle of the giant Sequoia trees of California requires many thousands of seasons (years) to evolve and unfold the inner pattern from seed to perfected tree, so does the much greater life-cycle of the Soul require many thousands

---

[1] *Realms of the Living Dead*, Curtiss, Chapter VII.

of "seasons" or life-cycles to bring its pattern into full manifestation, from seed to perfected Man, the Master, even when not constantly interfered with, retarded and pushed back by man's self-made Karma.

When we note the great prevalence of weakness, sickness and disease among mankind and the structural and functional imperfections of his body, we realize that in no other animal is its structure so poorly adapted to its posture as in man, even though the disadvantages of the upright position are enormously outweighed by the release of two limbs (arms) from the function of locomotion for the exclusive use of the brain and mind. The enormous influence upon the development of the brain and the greater mental power and intellectual attainments to which the use and development of the hand permitted expression, is well known to scientific investigators and psychologists. Yet no optical instrument so defective as the human eye, no automobile so inefficient as the body and no water-works or system of electrical conduits which allowed the leakage from one part to disable all its neighbors—as the inflammations and diseases of the abdominal and other organs leak or extend from one to the other through mere contact— would find a market in these days of efficiency.

When we consider the present imperfect organization of society, with its narrow racial outlooks and antagonisms and wars, its struggles between the so-called "classes," its extremes of great wealth and miserable poverty, how hopeless it all would be if we believed that these conditions were as near to the ultimate perfection of man as he could hope to attain! Yet in spite of all the imperfections in the Earth, in man's body and mental activities, and in his organization of society, we find a deep, eternal purpose and an ever-present urge, both in the Earth, in Nature and in man, toward something higher and better. Even the most undeveloped mentally and the most unawakened spiritually feel a dim Inner Urge toward higher unfoldment which, when once awakened, gives them no peace or rest until they begin to work with it.

Often, however, this Inner Urge is misinterpreted and man seeks to smother it out either through excessive self-indulgence of the lower appetites and passions, through a mad whirl of feverish social life or through incessant and strenuous mental activity, each according to his degree and type of development. But these attempts to smother out the cry of the inner or Spiritual Self for expression in the life only increase and make more persistent the conflict and inharmony, until finally the suffering which the rebellious personality brings upon itself forces it to appeal to the higher powers, commonly called God, for help. Then a new stage of evolution begins, *viz.*, the beginning of man's *conscious* recognition—howsoever dimly at first—of the Divine and his dependence upon It.

The second explanation is that in addition to the incompleteness of his present stage of evolution man also has to reap, express and work out the results of the Karma of his own creating as he goes along, *i.e.*, all the sin, sickness and inharmony that he has created in past lives and in the present, by the misuse of his creative powers and his God-given materials. For, until he recognizes and redeems his creations, and thereby learns the lesson, he will never cease creating such obstacles to his advance.

When man's creations are inharmonious and destructive in character, their working out and redemption naturally impedes and delays his evolution—the manifestation of the Spiritual Pattern—just as his creations of peace, harmony and purity accelerate it. Hence the Divine Self must wait patiently for all that man in his pompous ignorance, self-will and self-indulgence has created, to be worked out through the events of daily life, knowing well that if man will not listen to and strive to follow his Divine Guidance and live in harmony with the Divine Law, only the suffering which results from reaping that which he has sown and redeeming that which he has created, can turn his consciousness Godward and awaken him to the necessity of striving *consciously* to aid his spiritual unfoldment and thereby hastening the perfecting of his evolution.

God in His great love and mercy knows our imperfect and unfinished state and expects of us only the best we can do, each according to his lights. We could not expect a seedling to blossom and fruit ere it had become a tree. But we do expect it constantly to turn to the Sun, drink in the warm rain and assimilate the substances of the Earth and ultimately build all into perfect growth. And we delight in its upright stalk, in each tender leaf as it unfolds and in its every effort to grow aright. Just so God never expects His children to accomplish more than their particular stage of development and understanding permits. But He does expect us cheerfully and willingly to do our best, and He delights in our every effort.

God's Image, in which the Real Self is made, is not merely the cause which unfolds the pattern of the physical body, but it also focuses and outpictures the God-consciousness, the God-powers and the God-love of the Divine Father-Mother. And if man did not strive to correlate with the power of this Inner Self he would never realize his relation to nor his powers as a Son of the Father-Mother, and in appearance he would never be more than an ape-like creature.

A child inherits the traditions and mental traits, as well as the physical characteristics, of its family, but unless it strives to live up to and perfect those traits and traditions it is an unworthy representative of the family. "Further evolution, if it take place, cannot be an elemental and unconscious affair, but will result solely from *conscious efforts toward growth*. . . . Man, not striving toward evolution, not conscious of its possibility, *not helping it*, will not evolve. And the individual who is not evolving does not remain in a static condition, but goes down, *degenerates*. This is the general law."[2]

---
[2] *Tertium Organum*, Ouspensky, 329.

CHAPTER VII

MANIFESTING THE CREATION
(Concluded)

"Altho we accept the law of evolution, there is no necessity to regard all existing forms as having developed from one another.... In such cases it is more correct to regard them all as the *highest types in their own* evolution. The absence of intermediate forms makes this view much more probable than that which is usually accepted." *Tertium Organum*, Ouspensky, 336.

"Until we can grasp the sense of the reality, the greater importance, and beauty and satisfaction of the life of the Spirit—the life lived close to God—we are allowing material things to fetter us and rob as of the sweeter harmonies of life, rather than serve our highest good as they are designed to do." *The Seventh Seal*, Agnes, 98.

As we have already pointed out: We speak of the Divinity within, but in our present state of evolution that Divinity is scarcely more than the radiance of the emanations which the Divine Indweller left in-meshed in us when we were forced to leave the Garden when the mind usurped the authority of the spiritual will. But even this radiance is a very real Flame of spiritual force and through it we can always "ascend into the hill of the Lord" and reach the Indweller. Therefore, we must dwell in the thought of its radiant shining until it grows more and more intense; for through the misuse of mind we have driven it out, and by the proper use of mind we must bring it back. . . . In proportion as we turn the dynamic power of thought upon it, it will truly manifest in our outer lives, even in the outward appearance of the personality. It will bring to birth new powers, new strength, new health, new beauty, new love, new joy of life, new ability to help our fellowmen.[1]

Further to help in our spiritual unfoldment and our physical evolution we must discard all old ideas which the light of later understandings show to be imperfect or outgrown; for, as a rule, *change is an evidence of growth and progress*, while fixedness is stagnation and fossilization. Truly to progress we must consciously concentrate, not upon the physical body for the attainment of mere health, but upon the perfect completeness, symmetry and beauty of our Divine Self, and use all our creative powers to manifest that Divine Image in our flesh. Think of the Spiritual Body as a radiant Being within our flesh, a source of radiant spiritual life-force permeating our body and vivifying it with new life, just as radium does the Earth, that it shall find expression in greater health, cheerfulness and happiness. Rest in the calm assurance and unshakable faith that the radiance of that Divine Image will accomplish and take care of all the details of the needed results in the best possible way *if we permit it to do so*. Strive to be cheerful even during periods of depression (night-periods); for there is no real gain to be derived from giving way to depression or to

---

[1] *The Message of Aquaria, Curtiss*, 476, 472.

tears, since so often their seat is in self-pity.

During our final incarnations in the physical world, ere the Divine Image can shine thru in perfection, we have to pass thru a period during which the vibrations of every illness or weakness of the flesh which have been registered in the astral body have to be brought out and eliminated. This period of transmutation or house-cleaning is often one of great suffering, yet is an evidence that the time of our redemption and perfection draweth nigh. During the many house-cleanings thru which we have to pass, hold fast to the idea that the radiant life-force of the Divine Image is creating new and better conditions each day: new cells in the body, new ideas in the mind, new realizations in the Soul, and new conditions in the outer life; that it is constantly at work to manifest the perfection of the Spiritual Self.

Yet God has never left us comfortless. Always the power of the Holy Ghost has overshadowed us. And in our darkest hours the Flame of Divine Love has dwelt with us as a pillar of fire that has guided us thru the wilderness of life, and the Lord God has spoken to us out of the fiery cloud.

Because of the very brilliancy of this shining, man sees reflected on the darkness of his life his creations of sin and disobedience. Therefore, only as he seeks to embody and follow the guidance of the Divine Light which shines within can he learn how to advance to the point where he can re-enter his lost heritage, Eden.

Unless we often dwell in thought on the glorious

possibilities which the Light unfolds we cannot prepare ourselves to correlate with the Divine Indweller. Therefore, let each earnest reader who desires to have more than an intellectual knowledge of these truths; who desires to make a practical application of them, meditate upon the Divine Indweller[2] night and morning and as often as possible during the day, and visualize its manifestation within himself.

There never was or is an outer symbol, force or condition which does not have its corresponding inner mystic meaning or reaction in the life and consciousness of man. Just as radium always has been embodied in the Earth and sent out its transmuting and life-giving emanations to the planet and all mankind, so has the Christ-force[3] always been embodied in the heart of man and has striven to send out its life-giving emanations and its great powers of transmutation and redemption to the consciousness of the personality.

Just as comparatively few scientists of the past have recognized radium and its usefulness, so only the comparative few among the millions of mankind have consciously realized the presence of the Christ-force as a radiant center of the Divine within them. Only when man's evolution reached a point where he could understand and make proper use of radium for the good of all could he find it, altho advanced Souls in every age who had reached the necessary stage of

---

[2] See *The Message of Aquaria*, Curtiss, 477.
[3] See *Gems of Mysticism*, Curtiss, Chapter V.

evolution both knew about and utilized radio-active substances—as a kind of Philosopher's Stone—even if not pure radium.

Radium is one of the three-fold expressions of the Divine Life-force in the Earth, in this case in a metallic form. It is to the planet much like the Divine in man, *i.e.*, a source of radiant life-force. In another aspect it corresponds to Divine Mind which man's evolution is beginning to enable him to contact more consciously, just as his evolution is beginning to enable him to contact and utilize radium. And just as the Divine Mind must and does send out its radiant emanations thru the mortal mind, whether recognized or not, giving all thought-power a creative and persistent enduring force which enables it to accomplish concrete results, so does radium in the Earth give forth corresponding powers, constructive or destructive according to the degree and method of their use.

If our readers could once realize the destructively creative power of inharmonious, unkind and impure thoughts they would understand why there is so much evil in the world and why they have to fight so hard and so long. For evil thoughts are like pestiferous insects which breed in tremendous swarms, while good thoughts are more like the higher forms of life whose progeny are few and which must be nourished and cherished if they are to reproduce. How earnestly then should we strive to realize that the creative power of thought is the great step in evolution of the New Age in which it will be intensified many-fold, and that we must determine to use it constructively or the New

Age may be far worse than the past, because new and greater forces are being poured out for man for him to utilize.

Just as it requires but an infinitesimal particle of radium to produce a definite result, just so we, if we allow the Divine Light and Life to manifest thru and emanate from us, even though we may be infinitesimal in numbers, can help push on the evolution of both ourselves and all humanity and the planet itself. Thus can we each accomplish a definite and constructive work in the changing and chaotic conditions of today. For the Divine Law has made this period of evolution not merely the usual closing of one great cycle (the Piscean) and the beginning of a new (the Aquarian), but a special period when exceptional changes must come about.[4] This is a period when much that is old must be done away—old ways of thinking, acting, working, governing, doing business, worshipping, etc., that the evolution of all may be accelerated to keep pace with the other advances of the New Age.

We must adopt such new ideas, not merely in the form of outer creeds and dogmas of man's devising and sophistry, of condemnation or superiority over others whose ideas are slightly different, but we must look to the Divine Indweller to illumine our minds with a realization of our powers as a creator. Then our ability consciously to send forth powerful, positive and vital thoughts of peace, harmony, purity, brotherhood and co-operation will be a mighty factor in counteracting the mistakes and deficiencies of par-

---

[4] For details see *Coming World Changes*, Curtiss.

tially evolved man and his partially unfolded Spiritual Consciousness. For in spite of ourselves, and in spite of temporary set-backs, we are slowly evolving, since back of all our mistakes is the Urge to Good. But with our conscious co-operation and determined effort that evolving can be greatly accelerated and the suffering due to our ignorance and rebellion avoided.

As Samson[5] overcame the young lion barehanded and ate of the honey found in its carcass, so upon him who is strong in his faith in the Divine and who constantly looks to and relies upon It for guidance and help, will come "the spirit of the Lord mightily," so that out of danger shall come safety, out of inharmony brotherhood, out of competition co-operation, and out of that which seemed evil shall come sweetness and strength.

---

[5] *Judges*, XIV, 5-9.

CHAPTER VIII

ADAM AND EVE

"And the Lord said, It is not good that the man should be alone; I will make a help meet for him. . . . and He took one of his ribs. . . . and the rib, which the Lord God had taken from man, made He a woman, and brought her unto the man." *Genesis*, II, 18, 21-2.

"Only in relatively recent geological periods has the spiral course of cyclic law swept mankind into the lowest grade of physical evolution—the plane of material causation. . . . This took place in the middle of the Third Race, 18,000,000 years ago. . . . which embrace the duration of sexual, physical man." *The Secret Doctrine*, Blavatsky, II, 166.

Adam and Eve were not the first parents of all mankind. Even the *Bible* does not claim that. That was a Babylonian legend learned by the Hebrews during the long years of their captivity.[1] The *Bible* tells us that there were at least two other races on Earth at the same time with Adam and Eve, who were not their offspring. Firstly, there were the people of the land of Nod where Cain went and took unto himself a wife.

---

[1] "After the captivity, the Hebrew language was so little known to those who attended services in the Temple that, for 700 years, it was necessary for the High Priest to pause after the reading of each verse as it was given in Hebrew, in order that the interpreter might change it into the Chaldaic dialect or into Aramaic dialect, so that the listeners could understand what it was about!" *The Four-fold Process of God Creation*, Landone, I, 1.

(*Genesis*, iv, 16, 17.) Secondly, there was that mysterious race, called "the sons of God," which was apparently polygamous, for they "saw the daughters of men that they were fair; and they took them wives of *all which they choose.*" (*Genesis*, vi, 2.)

In fact, like most biblical narratives, the description is so worded as to divert those who give it any discriminating study from taking it literally. In addition to the wording of the text, the study of comparative religion now amply proves that Adam and Eve are not to be regarded as individual, historic personalities, but as types of the earliest physical race. As we have said elsewhere: The literal meaning of Adam is "red earth," hence Adam stands for the earthly Race of the Red Ray, red coming first because it is the lowest, most material vibration of the solar spectrum, the previous Races being too super-physical to be classed as earthly.[2]

While the allegorical story of Adam and Eve could not go into details, it nevertheless illustrates the descent of the Spiritual Man into Earth conditions, and the broad outlines of his subsequent evolution. Yet, if we are to "get wisdom, get understanding; forget it not," as Solomon enjoins us, we should know not only the broad outlines, but something of the details

---

[2] *The Message of Aquaria*, Curtiss, 77. "The first two races of men were too ethereal and phantom-like in their constitution, organism and *shape* even, to be called physical man. . . . this is one of the reasons why their relics can never be expected to be exhumed among other fossils." *The Secret Doctrine*, Blavatsky, II, 303.

of the marvelous process of *involution* or materialization of the invisible pattern of man into physical manifestation, as taught in Cosmic Philosophy, even tho those details may prove somewhat intricate and require more than a casual reading.

The Race referred to as Adam is represented quite correctly as being alone, for the first ethereal and only semi-materialized patterns were androgynous beings, containing both sexes in the one form, "male and female created he them." But as the descent into materialization³ reached the plane of dense physical matter, the manifestation necessarily had to conform to the laws of the physical plane. One of the most fundamental of these laws is the Law of Duality or Polarity. Under this Law all forces and manifestations on Earth must be separated into "pairs of opposites," or positive and negative, active and passive, expressions. Thus we have positive and negative, masculine and feminine, day and night, light and dark, heat and cold, summer and winter, etc. Under this Law the gradually materializing body was no longer sufficiently plastic for the expression of both sexes, hence they had to be differentiated into separate bodies, each specifically adapted for the expression of its sex.

Altho this process is represented in the condensed biblical allegory as an overnight affair, actually it was by no means a sudden change, but was the result of a gradual involution lasting throughout the entire latter

---

[3] For the details of the pre-physical conditions see chapter, "The Origin of Man," *The Voice of Isis*, Curtiss 228, 232-4.

half of the Third and the first part of the Fourth Great Races,[3] the first two Races being entirely super-physical. These primitive beings—of the first two Races—were still composed of semi-astral matter and today would not be visible. Therefore, they left no physical remains by which science might trace them. . . . Only later, toward the middle of the Third Race (Lemurian) did solid bones develop, the sexes separate, the body become clothed with "coats of skin" and take on human form as we know it today, altho at that time it was of gigantic proportions.[4]

As this separation of the sexes first took place during the super-physical involution of the astral patterns while still in the ethereal Eden, altho on their downward course into materialization, science finds no trace of a physically androgynous human Race, only the early separated materialized forms.

Their gigantic size is confirmed by *Genesis* (vi, 4), "there were giants in those days; and also after that." "It is not denied that. . . . [the body of] man was a gigantic *ape-like* creature; when we say 'man' we ought perhaps to say the rough mould that was developing for the use of [the spiritual man]. . . . Finally, it is shown in every ancient scripture and cosmogeny that man evolved primarily as a *luminous incorporeal form*, over which like molten brass poured into the model of a sculptor, the physical frame—or rather into the meshes of which—of his *body* was

---
[3] See footnote, page 83.
[4] *The Voice of Isis*, Curtiss, 232.

built by, through and from, the lower forms and types of animal terrestrial life."[5] This began to take place during the Mesozoic Age—the age of huge reptiles—when the bodies of all animal forms were of gigantic size. As we have already explained: These early types were gigantic semi-human monsters, the first attempt of material nature at building human bodies. . . . He is still gigantic and ethereal, but growing firmer and more condensed in body; a more physical man yet less intelligent, for mind is a slower and more difficult evolution than is the physical frame.[6]

The radio-active, refining and transmuting effect of a tremendously higher octave of vibrations brought to bear upon the gross and gigantic body by the introduction into it of self-consciousness—a far higher octave of vibration than animal mind—together with the effect of the still higher octave of vibrations coming from the newly incarnated "living soul," have progressively condensed that gross body, reduced its size and refined its structure until we now have the less gross, smaller but far more highly evolved body of modern man.

The process of the separation of the sexes is quite properly represented as a rib being taken from Adam's side, for the process at that time was one of budding, just as we see occur today in certain lower forms of life when the bi-sexual or androgynous stage passes directly into the stage of separate sexes in the suc-

---

[5] *The Secret Doctrine*, Blavatsky, II, 273; 118.
[6] *The Voice of Isis*, Curtiss, 231.

ceeding generations. According to Cosmic Philosophy: The emanations which came from their bodies during the seasons of procreation were ovulary; the small spherical nuclei, developing into a large, soft, egg-like vehicle, gradually hardened, when, after a period of gestation, it broke and the human animal issued from it unaided, as the fowls do in our Race; not a strange procedure when we remember that even today the now sexually generated child is born in a membraneous sack or large, soft, egg-like vehicle. . . . For in his physical development and in his modes of procreation man has passed thru all the stages Nature has used and still uses in the lower kingdoms,[7] as indisputably shown in the successive stages thru which the human embryo passes during intra-uterine life.

The truth that man can never be truly complete—hence can never do his best work—without his complementary mate is clearly indicated by Eve being taken from Adam's side. And he never can be truly complete until she is again blended with and becomes one with him, in purpose, ideals, mind and heart, if not in body. The biographies of most great men are almost unanimous in gladly attributing a large measure of their success to the inspiration, love and help of their mates.

The process by which the body of Eve was differentiated from that of Adam is therefore correctly described in general in the *Bible* story, even though it was not an actual rib that was used. This item is not

---

[7] *The Voice of Isis*, Curtiss, 231-2.

literal, but is as allegorical as the rest; for in the anatomy of man there is no rib missing. He has the same number on one side as on the other, and the same number as woman. What, then, is the significance of the use of the word rib? Why should that particular part of man's anatomy be mentioned as the origin of woman rather than any other?

The anatomy of the rib gives us the key to its symbolic interpretation. The ribs are an essential part of the framework of the body, without which the vital organs would not be protected or the body be able to maintain its erect posture. Here in one graphic word it is clearly indicated that woman was not created as a mere offshoot, as a mere appendage to man: as a possession of his or for man's mere companionship and pleasure, or as an after-thought of God's. This false interpretation by theologians was one of the major causes which for centuries kept woman in bondage and servitude, as a possession and chattel of man. But the obvious meaning of the symbol indicates that woman is not an appendage, but *an integral part of the body of humanity* and the framework of society, without which its vital organs would not be protected or humanity be able to maintain its uprightness. Under the Law of Duality woman is but the natural differentiation of the feminine aspect of the one Spiritual Being in the Spiritual World who is seeking manifestation on Earth through the two co-equal masculine and feminine organisms.

Sex, therefore, is not merely a thing of the body,

but inheres in the Soul itself.[8] It also inheres in every differentiated or individualized form of consciousness long before it manifests in the flesh. In fact it manifests in the flesh only because it already exists in the pre-physical pattern of which the flesh is but a materialization.

This same law applies to woman's mind as well as to her body. For while woman's mind is of the intuitive type, able to grasp the essence of truth without the laborious process of logical reasoning required to reach the same truth by man's rational type of mind, her mind is in no way inferior to man's. Even in the structure of woman's brain, the critical examination of the brain of the celebrated feminist, Helen Gardner, by the neurological specialists at Cornell University shows that: "Compared in each of its details with the brains of twenty other men and women, the brain of Mrs. Gardner has presented abundant evidence that the brain of a woman need not be inferior to that of a man of equal rank. In its entire structure it reveals a wealth of cortical substance, or gray matter, that is only equaled, but not exceeded, by the best brains in the Cornell collection, which includes those of a number of doctors, professors, lawyers and naturalists."[9]

While the brain structures of men and women are comparable, their types of mind are as distinctive

---

[8] For the geometrical proof see *The Key to the Universe*, Curtiss, 349.
[9] Dr. James W. Papez, *New York Times*, Oct. 9, 1927.

as their types of body. They are not alike and were never intended to be alike: they are complements each of the other. And both, working harmoniously together, are needed for the highest manifestation of the Soul-consciousness in society, or the outer affairs of mankind.

As we have said elsewhere of woman during this coming age: Adam, or the Real or Divine Self, will once more give up a mental "rib" or a part of the framework of his mental body and out of it will be fashioned once more a help-meet for him. In other words, during the past ages of the world it has been man who has built up the mental conceptions and ideals which have influenced, moved and controlled the religious, business and social fabric of society, while woman has had her place in the intellectual and spiritual background, hidden within the body of man, so to speak, altho always an important upholder of the structure of the man-made society. But in this coming Woman's Age, now dawning, she will take her place as a co-equal part of the framework of human society, no longer merely a rib in a man's world, but having ribs and a complete independent structure of her own, which shall henceforth work as a co-equal with man in bringing forth the new conditions for humanity.[10]

Since the special and specific organization of woman's body necessarily makes her open to the higher invisible worlds that she may give incarnation to the

---

[10] *The Message of Aquaria*, Curtiss, 78.

Souls in those worlds which desire birth into the physical world, so should she be open to and bring down to Earth and give embodiment to such higher spiritual ideals as love, compassion, purity, righteousness and joy which are seeking incarnation in the minds and lives of humanity. Her relation to man should be to stimulate his passion for Truth instead of his passion for lust. Her greatest aim should be to lead man not to the altar, but to idealism. She should strive not for political but for moral and spiritual leadership. In other words, woman's mission on Earth is to represent the Divine Mother in spiritual things as she does now in physical things: to give embodiment and physical manifestation to ideals as she now gives embodiment and physical manifestation to incarnating Souls.

According to tradition it was the fifth rib on the left side that was used to fashion Eve. This too has a wonderful symbology, for that is the rib which covers or encloses the heart, the universal symbol of the feminine or heart qualities or love-nature—intuition, sympathy, compassion, etc. This indicates that in woman there is a greater and more independent expression of the divine love nature of the Soul than there could possibly be in an androgynous being dominated by the masculine aspect. "Until this cycle in the world's history, almost every system of religion and esoteric philosophy has rejected the feminine, and either taught the absolute separation of the sexes as the ideal—segregating women in convents and men in monasteries—or has in some way rejected woman, even to the extent of denying to woman a Soul and barring her from Paradise except to minister to man's desires."[11]

"The time has now come when woman must take her place as the Priestess of the Most High, the Revealer of Purity and Truth to man.... It is woman who must lift up the world's ideas of the sex-force from the mire and degradation of man's misconceptions and give this great power its proper place in the Temple of the Living God (the body) as the highest expression of the Divine in man. Just as it was woman who gave to man the apple of discord, so must it be woman who plucks the golden apples that grow at the top of the Tree of Life and gives them to man to eat.... But, until woman awakens to her responsibility and understands her real mission, *i.e.*, her power to play upon man's heart, stimulate his noblest aspirations and thus lead him to the heights of spiritual attainment, instead of into mere physical union without love, she will continue to be the slave she is today, in spite of any political or social liberties she may attain."[12]

Man is as ready today as ever to be led by woman in any altruistic and unselfish crusade, but to secure his co-operation he must be led by ideals, for he instinctively resists being driven by force or compulsion. Most women realize this power of moral leadership, but they should understand that it is their duty, their great privilege and their great opportunity.

---

[11] The Voice of Isis, Curtiss, 336.
[12] The Voice of Isis, Curtiss, 253-5.

As woman today begins to awaken to her independent status, her first reaction is to think that to be man's equal she must do the things he does and copy him as much as possible. She therefore endeavors to suppress all normal contours and strives for a boyish figure, boyish bob, boy-scout hiking clothes and so forth. She even apes his bad habits and vices, smoking on the streets and in automobiles, drinking in public, etc. Yet, at the same time, to attain her own ends she continues her age-old efforts to fascinate and enslave man by her scanty and suggestive dress, her facial make-up and her general "sex appeal." In all this, instead of exhibiting her independence, she tacitly confesses that there is a superiority in man worthy of imitation. She thereby reveals the "inferiority complex" which her ages of subjection by man has built into the race consciousness.

If we did not know that all this is but an exuberant phase of the first stages of her newly won freedom — much as children run, shout and throw up their caps when let out of school — we might well fear for her future. But we know that ere long she will drop these essentially unfeminine fads and begin to express the higher and more worthy aspects of true feminism.

It is not so long ago that man passed thru a similar stage, aping woman by dressing in effeminate, lace trimmed clothes, seeking to gain distinction by the shape of his legs, exposing his knees, using face powder and rouge, carrying lace handkerchiefs and jeweled snuffboxes, and doing everything to express his vanity of person and increase his "sex-appeal."

And if man has learned that real superiority is not exhibited by clothes or personal adornment, but by the expression of superior qualities of mind and heart, so must woman learn the same lesson. The "superiority complex" that each must attain is to rise superior to the usual faults and weaknesses of the less evolved. For, to be truly equal, men and women must strive to express the highest possibilities of true manhood and true womanhood and not give way to passing weakness and fads which only reveal the vanity of a Soul not yet awakened to the higher conceptions of life.

To reach his highest expression of life a man must recognize not merely woman's true position in society and co-operate with her in all constructive and uplifting endeavors, but he must learn to recognize and develop the feminine qualities—sympathy, intuition, compassion and love—within himself, just as woman must learn to balance her feminine qualities with the masculine qualities of logic, reason, courage and will, ere humanity as a whole can bring forth its highest ideals.

CHAPTER IX

THE GARDEN IN EDEN

"And the Lord planted a garden eastward in Eden; and there he put the man whom he had formed. And out of the ground made the Lord God to grow every tree that is pleasant to the sight, and good for food; the tree of life also in the midst of the garden, and the tree of knowledge of good and evil." *Genesis*, II, 8-9.

"The student of Occultism has to bear in mind that every God and hero in ancient Pantheons (that of the *Bible* included) has three biographies in the narrative, so to say, running parallel with each other and each connected with one of the aspects of the hero -historical, astronomical and perfectly mythical, the last serving to connect the other two together and smooth away the asperities and discordances of the first two." *The Secret Doctrine*, Blavatsky, III, 94.

Probably in no other chapters of the *Bible* is the manifest absurdity of the words, when taken in their literal and materialistic sense, so evident as in the first four chapters of *Genesis*.[1] It is imaginatively possible to conceive of a god taking a handful of clay and modeling an image of man, animating it and later on marshaling the more than 1,000,000 species of living things—including 3,500 species of mammals, 3,500 species of reptiles, 400,000 species of insects, etc.—in a long line which would reach across four states from New York City to Washington, D.C.,

---

[1] See *The Voice of Isis*, Curtiss, 75.

and parading them before that newly animated mannikin that he might name them (*Genesis*, ii, 19). But to accomplish this God would have to keep them all in line, prevent their fighting or straying, supply them with their specific foods and keep them stepping forward at the rate of one each minute of the day for *nearly four years*, supposing that Adam could inspect, understand and correctly name a new species *each minute* for twelve hours a day without stopping for meals or to rest his voice; for at that time he was alone among all the animals and had no Eve to bring him food. During this four years all the larger animals would have brought forth several generations of progeny, while the lower forms—many of which have a life-cycle of only a few hours or days—would have reproduced in countless swarming millions. The absurdity of a literal interpretation is too obvious to merit discussion.

Even if we grant the possibility of so great a miracle, it is a little too much for the literalists to ask us to believe in a serpent that can talk, a tree that confers immortal life and another tree that can teach man the knowledge of good and evil. All of which is quite as allegorical and fabulous as any mythology or so-called "heathen" scripture asks us to accept.

According to St Augustine—one of the four great authorities and leaders among the early Church Fathers, and the one who largely formulated and gave the Christian doctrines their traditional trend—says:

"There is no way of preserving the literal sense of the first chapters of Genesis without impiety and attributing things to God unworthy of him."[2] It should therefore be fairly obvious that the *Bible* is purposely written in symbolic and allegorical language so absurd in its literal sense as to force mankind to seek some other interpretation. As St Paul tells us: "The letter killeth, but the spirit giveth life."[3] It is just this spiritual interpretation which we endeavor to present in this and the other volumes of "The Curtiss Books." As we have pointed out: To be efficient in life's day at school a philosophy should be sought which is so all-inclusive that it explains where we come from, why we are here, what the destiny is to which we are expected to reach, and what our individual place is in the whole mighty scheme of the universe, and how we are to attain it.[4] The essentials of this Cosmic Spiritual Philosophy have been known to the illumined Seers, Adepts, Wise Men and Initiates into the Mysteries in all ages, but have been withheld from the profane who could not understand them without the special training that is given to a Candidate for the Mysteries. As St. Augustine plainly tells us: "What is *now* called the Christian religion has existed among the ancients, and *was not absent from the beginning of the human race* until Christ came in the flesh, from which time true

---

[2] *Retractions*, St. Augustine, I, 13.
[3] *II Corinthians*, III, 6.
[4] *The Message of Aquaria*, Curtiss, 186.

religion, *which already existed*, began to be called Christian."[5]

The locality of the Garden of Eden has been vainly sought, not only by Christian theologians, but also by religionists of all creeds, from the days of the early Indian Aryans to the present day; for the story of a Garden as the birthplace of humanity is by no means confined to the Christian Scriptures. The Hindoo legend of such an Elysium or Paradise is still more striking. "In the sacred mountain *Meru*, which is perpetually clothed in the golden rays of the Sun, and whose lofty summit reaches into heaven, no sinful man can exist. It is guarded by a dreadful dragon. It is adorned with many celestial plants and trees, and is watered by four rivers which separate and flow to the four chief directions."[6] Among the Hindoos the Garden is located near the Lake of the Dragon in the plateau of Pamir, from which region go forth the four rivers, Ozus, Indus, Ganges and the Silo. Among the Greeks there were also four symbolic rivers, but these were represented as being in the nether world or the plane of physical embodiment, namely, the *Phlegethon*, *Cocytus*, *Styx* and *Acheron*, whose symbology we have described elsewhere.[7] Cuneiform inscriptions have also been found which show conclusively that the Babylonians had this legend 15,000 years before the Hebrews. Of this legend of a garden we are told:

---

[5] *Retractions*, St. Augustine, I, 13.
[6] *The Pentateuch Examined*, Colenso, IV, 153.
[7] *The Key to the Universe*, Curtiss, 149-150.

"It was born in that mysterious locality which no one is able to locate, and which is the despair of both Geographers and Christian Theologians."[8] Therefore let us try to grasp the main lesson which this most ancient and universal myth outpictures, and deduce from the *Bible* narrative of it some logical sequence and helpful application.

The statement that the Garden was placed "east-ward in Eden" is significant. On a rotating globe there can be no spot that is actually, only relatively, east or west. A particular spot can be east or west only from some point arbitrarily chosen according to a conventional division of the Earth's surface. Even today, to the people of the Far East, America lies east of them, although it is called the Western World.

Placing the Garden "eastward in Eden" does not locate it in the least, and hence *no such spot has ever been found*. The *Encyclopedia Britannica* tells us that "research into primitive beliefs, guided by the comparative method, leads to the view that the 'Garden' was originally a celestial (super-physical) locality.... the geographical details given in the *Bible* are rather difficult to work into a consistent picture."[9] As a matter of fact, it was purposely intended that no such spot was ever to be located and found *literally and physically*, for the entire narrative is symbolic. The supposed location varies with each racial story of creation, Babylonian, Chaldean, Mayan, Incan, etc.

---

[8] *The Secret Doctrine*, Blavatsky, III, 94.
[9] Vol. VIII, 923.

Therefore, we may well exclaim with Origen, one of the greatest authorities among the Fathers of the early Christian Church, "What man is found such an idiot as to suppose that God planted trees in Paradise, in Eden, like a husbandman?"[10]

Since the Spiritual Man was created in the higher super-physical worlds like "every plant of the field before it was in the earth, and every herb of the field before it grew," the Eden in which this Man was placed symbolizes the super-physical, ethereal globe which was condensing from radiant matter through the stage of fire-mist into a physical or dense material Earth. Eden also symbolizes the state of innocence and spiritual consciousness which the Soul enjoyed before it was embodied in matter. And man cannot return to or re-enter this Eden until he has mastered matter, learned to rule his Garden, and has so purified and spiritualized the body through which he manifests that it can vibrate to the high octave of Edenic conditions. This is the goal of all his evolution through matter.

The bare statement about the formation of man is first elaborated as a mystical allegory; we are told that first Eden is formed and then within it a Garden is fashioned, and in the Garden is placed "the man," or more correctly the "living Soul." What is more reasonable than to understand that this Garden, made of the dust of the Earth and planted and watered and fitted in every way as a dwelling place for the "living

---

[10] *Mystery of Adoni*, 176.

soul" who had come to incarnate on the Earth through the Divine Breath, was this same *body* of man referred to in the previous verse, man's semi-astral or etherealized body; that newly individualized portion or "Garden"? It was a concrete, individualized portion of the newly created globe of universal primordial substance or fire-mist which, through cosmic involution, had taken on the form of the new planet, Earth, here called Eden.

Since the east is the point where the Sun rises to give light, life and warmth to the physical world, it is used in the symbolical and allegorical writings in all languages to symbolize *the point of origin* of all things, the super- or pre-physical, the Spirit. Therefore, when man's body (the Garden) began to manifest physically on Earth out of the previously invisible ethereal state, since man's destiny is to be the Light-Bearer and Ruler of the globe, it was quite correct to describe it as appearing "eastward in Eden," just as the Sun appears in the east out of the mists of night to illumine and rule the day.

As we have already pointed out: In *Genesis*[11] we find four mystical rivers represented as watering the Garden of Eden—*Pison, Gigon, Hiddekel* and *Euphrates*. Taking Eden as a symbolic reference to the body of man, these four rivers correspond to the four great arteries proceeding from the heart, which carry the purified blood to the four regions of the body indicated. The first river, *Pison*—whose meaning is

---

[11] II, 10-14.

"joined together as one"—which "compasseth the whole land of Havilah," refers to the innominate artery which is formed by the right subclavian and the right common carotid arteries "joined as one." The meaning of the word Havilah is "to bring forth; to form, create; to supply strength," all of which vividly portrays the offices of the brain and right arm and head, which are supplied by this river of blood. The river *Gihon*—signifying "to run out; to burst forth into thought"—refers to the left common carotid artery which supplies the left side of the brain and head. The third river, *Hiddekel*—meaning "freely flowing"—refers to the left subclavian artery which supplies the left arm. The fourth river, *Euphrates*—meaning "to increase; the creative power; the fruitful river," etc.—symbolizes the descending aorta, the great river of blood that supplies the lungs and the entire body below the diaphragm, including the creative centers. Thus the four rivers "water" the whole Garden.[12]

With this basic conception in mind it is easy to discern the meaning of the seemingly ridiculous incident of the animals being brought to Adam to be named. For since the *body* of man is the result of the evolution of all the lower kingdoms, every child that is born inherits not only all the functions developed by the animal kingdom, but also embodies the cream of all the experiences passed through during all previous stages of evolution. As the physical body or material

---

[12] *The Key to the Universe*, Curtiss, 149-150.

manifestation of the Earth was evolved long before the body of man appeared upon it, so was the body of man evolved long before his Soul descended and appeared within it. And since his body was formed of earth materials it necessarily has within it all the development that the earth particles have attained. Man's body, therefore, contains the synthesized essence of all the instincts, tendencies and potentialities of all the lower kingdoms—the vegetable, the animal, the birds and every creeping thing. These are all transmuted into faculties, functions, powers and instinctive reactions of body and mind, as evidenced by the stages through which the body passes before birth.

Not only do we inherit the potentialities of the lower kingdoms, but we embody many of the actual atoms that composed their bodies. This is evidenced by the fact that man's body is formed of the dust of the ground. And of what is that dust composed? Through countless ages all prehistoric forms of life had to have their evolution and leave their remains behind. Through still greater ages these remains had to be consolidated in the sedimentary rocks, oil shale, etc. Then as the sedimentary rocks disintegrated into dust in succeeding ages, they released the very atoms that composed the bodies of all the prehistoric forms of life, from the tiny trilobite to the hundred foot *Atlantosauris*, the giant *Baluchetherium* and the *Dinosaur*. Even of man today it is said, "Dust thou art and unto dust shalt thou return."

The dust also contains the remains of all the later

forms of life that have ever manifested on Earth, many of the same atoms of which are built into man's body. For from the soil they are built into the plants, grains, fruits and animals which man uses for food and so become a part of his body, as they became a part of the bodies of many previous forms of life. And since every atom bears the radio-active imprint of every dynamic form of life with which it has been intimately associated, our bodies not only inherit the functions and instincts of the lower kingdom, but actually possess the same atoms and radio-active emanations."[13] In fact, we have within us every element that has entered into the formation and evolution of the planet and all that ever dwelt thereon. Yet out of this dust of the ages, which contained all the imperfections of the earlier stages and all the impurities of the earlier forms, out of all this refuse the Lord God saw fit to evolve a body which the Spiritual Man would have to use as his instrument thru which to manifest on Earth and which he must ultimately so purify and perfect as to enable him to become the Lord of Creation and the Ruler of the Garden.

This conception also gives the key to that other similar miracle of Noah gathering two of every kind of beast, bird and reptile into the ark. For in one sense the ark symbolizes the human fetus floating in the amniotic waters while it repeats or embodies all the animals or the lower stages of evolution. If it would have taken Adam nearly four years merely

---

[13] For further details, see *The Message of Aquaria*, Curtiss, 255.

to name the different species when already gathered and brought to him, how long would it have taken Noah to roam the Earth, after the rains had begun and many parts were already under water, and capture, feed and transport to the ark, two of every kind of bird, reptile and animal? It is evident that the symbolic interpretation is the only possible one.

As we have previously explained: To interpret, through the science of Logography, the story of the naming of the animals means that man must take all the materials and animal forces to be found in his body, recognize the good they can accomplish for him, and gather up their true essence of life and build it into his higher Soul-life. Herein lies one of the greatest mysteries of life, for not only is man given dominion over all these kingdoms, but he assumes his dominion only as he "names," *i.e.*, recognizes, controls and gives them their true place in the Garden or uplifts them in his own organism."[14]

This incident of naming the animals gives marvelous proof of the power and place of intuition—tuition from within—or the ability of properly trained Seers to receive revelations from superior Beings. For at the time the *Bible* was compiled there were no written records as to what took place in Eden thousands of years before, nor was there any physical science or even any scientific instruments for the investigation of Nature. Hence there were no palaeontological or anthropological data from which to deduce a theory

---

[14] *The Message of Aquaria*, Curtiss, 256-7.

of evolution. Yet the general outline of the entire scheme was so fully grasped and so clearly understood that the whole process was marvelously and correctly expressed in that one pregnant verse. (*Genesis*, ii, 19.)

Altho man is the crowning point of evolution, he is still more or less affected by all the lower forces which he embodies, and he must learn to master and control them ere he can become the Lord of Creation. For as long as he allows the inherent characteristics of the minerals and chemical activities of the Earth, the gases of the air, the herbs of the field; the traits, powers and instincts of the beasts, the birds and the creeping things, to sway him, he is still the slave of physical conditions. Because of this there is a certain amount of truth in the theories of determinism and behaviorism.

But if even one man ever surmounted the handicaps his heredity and environment placed upon him, he has proved that determinism is not a compelling law; that while heredity and environment have a noticeable influence on his career, they are, nevertheless, only minor factors. The major and essential factor is the degree of advancement of the incarnating Soul; for its degree of unfoldment will manifest, no matter what the heredity and environment.

The fact that poor and uneducated boys of obscure parents overcome all obstacles of heredity and environment and rise to be presidents of banks, railroads, steel trusts, etc., while their brothers and sisters, born under exactly the same conditions, do not rise out of their environmental influences, plainly shows that it is the inherent quality of Soul that is the determining factor and not heredity and environment. Abraham Lincoln was born with the heredity and in an environment of a "rail splitter" and ninety-nine out of one hundred of the others in that environment remained "rail splitters" because they were not advanced Souls. But Lincoln was an advanced Soul and he demonstrated his greatness of Soul by overcoming all handicaps and expressing the degree of his spiritual advance in spite of all deterministic factors.

Once we recognize that *we are more than mere human animals* reacting to the conditions in our environment and to our inbred animal instincts; that we have within us all the powers and potencies of the "living Soul," the Spiritual Man, with which to rule our Garden, we need no longer be subject to the rule of the lower vibrations, but are capable of ruling over them in love and wisdom.

The Soul comes down from the higher worlds pure and perfect and is given its Garden in which to dwell. God made this Garden perfect and filled it with all needful trees and fruits, but through many incarnations man has only too often scattered the seeds of weeds in his Garden, many of which proved poisonous. He also planted many trees of whose bitter fruit he must eat until he learns that they should have no place in his Garden. The Lord God instructed man to tend and cultivate his Garden, perfect its fruits and rule over all its inhabitants and manifestations, and man must reincarnate again and again until he has accomplished his mission and taken his place as the Lord of Creation.

"Once this new idea is recognized by the mind, according to the laws of mind there is a modification of the mind in conformity with the idea. And if the idea is held continually or is recurred to frequently and positively, it grows and grows and reacts upon the body with greater and greater power until finally the body is modified in conformity with the new idea, just as was the mind. This is true of the birth of every new conception in proportion to the power we give it. . . . We must, therefore, seriously face ourselves and *cease our opposition* to the manifestation of the Divine in us; must learn what our Real Self is and what influences come from It and what from the lower personal self. . . . It is this struggle for the manifestation of the Image projected from the consciousness of God when we were sent forth on our cycle of evolution, that is destined to unfold the perfect pattern and fill a certain place in the Grand Plan."[15] Once this is realized then will all these subjects of ours be brought to our attention by the Lord (Law), as they are represented as being brought to Adam, to be recognized and named, and to serve us and worship at our feet as Lord of the Garden.

The body, then, is the Garden given each incarnated Soul to cultivate and rule. It is filled with all kinds of

---

[15] *The Message of Aquaria*, Curtiss, 421-2, 368.

plants (vegetative functions) and trees (nerve trunks and their forces, also fruits of the Spirit), "both pleasant to the sight and good for food," which the "living Soul" must tend, cultivate and ultimately bring to perfection. It is also swarming with "every fowl of the air (thoughts and ideas) and every beast of the field" (appetites, passions and desires) which the Lord (Law) brings to the attention of "the man" to be recognized as being within and a part of himself, and to be named, controlled and trained to follow the Law ere "the Man" can re-enter and ultimately become the ruler of Eden, as the Lord of Creation.

CHAPTER X

THE TREES IN THE GARDEN

"Out of the ground made the Lord God to grow every tree that is pleasant to the sight, and good for food; the Tree of Life also in the midst of the garden, and the Tree of Knowledge of good and evil." *Genesis*, II, 9.

"What man is found such an idiot as to suppose that God planted trees in Paradise, in Eden, like a husbandman?"*Mystery of Adonai*, St. Augustine, 176.

In the previous chapters we have seen that Eden embraced far more than merely a Garden, for Eden was the entire newly created ethereal globe[1] in which all things were still in the perfection of their astral patterns—"every plant of the field before it was in the earth, and every herb of the field before it grew"—as yet unmodified, limited or distorted by embodiment in the densest state of physical matter. The tiny Garden was man's etherealized and as yet pure body in which the Real or androgynous Man dwelt before the sexes separated and he became truly terrene. Each Soul incarnating on this planet has given to it, as the materials for its dwelling place, just such a Garden or as much of the physical substance of the planet as is necessary for its formation and maintenance. Since man is the crowning creation or the ultimate of evo-

---
[1] For details see *The Voice of Isis*, Curtiss, 204.

lution on this globe, he must ultimately become its ruler.

According to one authority[2] the Hebrew word translated "Garden" comes from a root-word which means *enveloped* as with a mantle. This root-meaning is found not only in the Hebrew, but in the Sanskrit and Egyptian. It has no reference at all to a physical place or garden, but refers to the Spiritual Man "enveloped" in astral or semi-physical matter.

The consciousness of the human animal in which the Soul is now enveloped responds more readily to the vibrations from its animal nature and to the vibrations from the physical world, which come thronging into it through the avenues of its five senses, and these vibrations naturally tend to awaken desires for the things from which they come. The enveloping of the Soul in a crude material body greatly lessens its response to spiritual vibrations and it begins to listen more to the call of the flesh than to the inner voice of the Lord God which speaks within its Garden. In other words, it begins to be ruled by the outer vibrations instead of by the vibrations from the Real or Spiritual Man. Thus do the bodily senses seduce man to transgress the Law, the results of which eventuate in his expulsion from the Garden.

In the light of this interpretation we see that the Tree of Life in the midst of the Garden is the spinal cord whose sap is referred to later[3] as the River of

---

[2] Brown Landone.
[3] *Revelation*, XXII.

THE TREES IN THE GARDEN 111

Life. At the present stage of evolution only the physiological, and the beginnings of the psychological, functions of this marvelous "tree" are developed in the average man. But it contains mystical and spiritual centers[4] which are more or less dormant as yet, like the tightly rolled buds of a rose. Yet this mysterious Tree can bear good fruit only when it has reached a mature stage of evolution. Its fruit can ripen normally only in the light of the Spiritual Sun and not in the reflected light of the astral world where there are so many deceptive lights and fearsome shadows: so many misleading and evil forces ever ready to blight the fruit in the bud or cause perverted and abnormal development. Through the ultimate development of this Tree and its fruit, in some far-distant stage of evolution, the body of man will acquire much higher functions and powers, and as a result it will become so spiritualized and responsive to the radio-activity of the indwelling Spiritual Man that he will evolve above the present state of the human kingdom into the super-human kingdom by the acquisition and utilization of those spiritual powers, just as he has evolved out of the animal kingdom into the human or super-animal kingdom, by the acquisition and utilization of the added powers of a "living soul."

What will eventually result when this mystical Tree of Immortal Life, mentioned in the first chapters of the *Bible*, is partaken of, is repeatedly set forth in the

---

[4] Connected with the seven nerve plexuses – sacral, prostatic, solar, cardiac, laryngeal, pharyngeal and cavernous.

Bible from *Genesis* to *Revelation*. In *Genesis* we are told of the Tree of Life in the midst of the garden before the sexes were separated, while in *Revelation*[5] the picture of the perfected attainment of the separated sexes is represented as the Tree of Life "on either side of the river [which] yielded her fruit every month; and the leaves of the tree were for the healing of the nations." In fact all that transpires between the first chapters and the last may be interpreted as a grand allegory of the Path of Attainment which the Soul has to tread from the time of its first incarnation in a human-animal body until it completes its Cycle of Necessity and reaches at-one-ment with the Father in the Holy City of the New Jerusalem in the superphysical worlds. Then the River of Life[5] shall flow, out of the throne of God, that is, it shall no longer be a current of physical life-force, but of spiritual life-force flowing from the Spiritual Man into all his bodies.

With this basic conception in mind we can see how historic personages, places and events have been woven into the story—often quite out of their actual setting—to illustrate the truths intended. The many unjustified wars, seizures of property and expulsions of whole nations from their homelands; the cruelties and injustices apparently not only sanctioned, but commanded by Jehovah were but intended to illustrate the conquering, subjugating or expelling of the lower traits, passions and desires of the animal-man that

---

[5] *Revelation*, XXII, 1-2.

THE TREES IN THE GARDEN 113

the Lord God might reign. When this is realized, much of the sting is taken out of many otherwise unanswerable modern historical criticisms.

If all such events are taken literally we cannot blame sincere scholars, whose sense of justice and humanity is outraged by the apparent sanction of such things, for exclaiming: "Yahweh was a strange god, a god of battles, a god of torture, a god unwilling to forgive his erring creatures without an oblation of blood. He connived with his favorites at trickery, thieving, and murder. He pursued those he disliked with relentless hatred. He avowed himself a just god and dispensed injustice. He preached love and stirred up hatred."[6] All of which is undeniable in the face of a literal interpretation. This writer simply does not understand that the *Bible* must be spiritually discerned and not literally interpreted. For all the terrible things he complains of become entirely justifiable as an allegory of the struggles of the Soul to manifest the Image of God amidst the warring instincts of the flesh.

However, since this volume is not the place for an exposition of this theme, we merely mention it in passing.*

But there is another tree in the midst of the Garden, which grows from the roots of the Tree of Life. The fruit of this second tree, the orthodox translation tells us, man was warned not to eat lest he die. This was

---

[6] *The Forum*, October, 1927, 533-4.
* For further details see "The Curtiss Books," especially *The Message of Aquaria*, *The Voice of Isis*, etc.

the Tree of Knowledge. Knowledge of what? Since man already possessed the knowledge of the spiritual worlds, this new knowledge against which he was warned must have been knowledge concerning the new world into which he was destined to descend, the world of materiality ruled by the Law of Duality, the world in which would be found all the "pairs of opposites," good and evil, etc. And since the Tree of Immortal Life represents the immortal Ray of the Divine Monad, it can be approached in consciousness only by eating of the Tree of Knowledge by which alone intelligence and discrimination can be developed, even though this involves partaking of the bitter fruit of personal experience—pain, suffering and disappointment.

Man's spiritual parents warned him that as he partook of the fruit of this tree or gained a knowledge of materiality he would become so enmeshed in matter and the limitations it would impose on the Spirit that he would surely die to the consciousness of the spiritual world, just as our consciousness today dies or ceases to react to the spiritual world as we are born into the physical world. For ere the Soul can reincarnate on Earth it must drink of the Cup of Lethe—the Cup of Forgetfulness—and forget its heavenly home as it once more takes up its unfinished tasks, learns its new lessons and unfolds new powers in the physical world.

But the Great Initiator or Serpent of Wisdom told man that he would not *surely* or completely die to the higher knowledge, but that ultimately his spiritual eyes would be opened to know both the spiritual and the

THE TREES IN THE GARDEN

material worlds and thus become "as gods," knowing both extremes. For he must know both the spiritual and the material, the unlimited and the limited, the good and the limitation of good or the relatively evil, ere he can become the Lord of Creation and properly tend and rule his Garden.

One aspect of the Tree of Knowledge of Good and Evil, is the lower human mind of the personality or the intellect. Its product or fruit is composed of the vibrations from the outer physical world coming into it thru the five physical senses and producing or giving rise to or recognizing and responding to the sensations, appetites and desires of the animal body, and often engendering, in the more advanced, self-aggrandizement and pride of intellect. To be ruled by these vibrations, instead of by the vibrations from the Real or Spiritual Man, brings about transgressions of the Law which eventuate in death. For "the man" Adam is "born an image of clay, into which the 'Lord God' breathes the breath of life, but *not of intellect* and discrimination, which are developed only after he had tasted of the fruit of the Tree of Knowledge; in other words, when he has acquired the first development of Mind, whose terrestrial aspect is of the earth earthy, although its highest faculties connect it with Spirit and the Divine Soul."[7] While the earliest type of man who had only just become self-conscious could not become intellectually discriminating until after he had eaten of the fruit of the Tree of Knowledge thru

---
[7] *The Secret Doctrine*, Blavatsky, II, 185.

experience in the conditions of material embodiment, he should have done so under the guidance of the incarnating Soul and not thru the guidance of the animal desires.

According to the Hebrew scholar already quoted[8] the Hebrew word translated "tree" (*Ets*) really means growth, growing or growth toward attainment. The fruit of this growth is represented in the *Bible* story as a knowledge of good and evil. But the word translated "knowledge" (*Daath*) also means knowing. The word for "good" (*Tob*) also means cheer and joy; while the word translated "evil" is the Egyptian root *Ra*, meaning the "life-giver." Therefore the real meaning of the sentence is "growth in knowledge of the life-giver or the life-giving power." What is this life-giving or creative power of which Adam and Eve were told not to eat lest they die?

As we have already explained: According to the same symbology this Tree which is in the midst of the Garden is the spinal cord, the sap of which is the kundalini-force (serpent-force), a dynamic, *creative* power functioning through the spinal cord, its lower aspect of creativeness being expressed through the sex organs and its higher aspect ultimately functioning through the pineal gland. The fruit of this tree is the spiritual power gained as a result of the opening of that which is known as the Third Eye. As man, through experience, gains Wisdom he uses this mystic power gradually to bring about its higher physical

---

[8] *The Four-fold Process of God Creation*, Landone, IV, 3.

manifestations, as well as the psychic and spiritual.[9] When normally awakened, as a result of spiritual growth, "it slowly ascends the spinal cord through the central canal until it reaches and stimulates into activity the pineal gland, the *conscious* functioning of which is called the opening of the Eye of Wisdom.... through which the disciple is able to see the 'glory of the Lord' surrounding him. This is a physical effect which accompanies spiritual illumination."[9]

Since the unfoldment of this spiritual bud and the *conscious* use and control of this spiritually creative power is one of the ultimate attainments of that higher evolution which will enable man to become Super-man, at their present stage of evolution it remains dormant in the masses of mankind.

Man cannot become Super-man until he has reached an advanced stage of spiritual development and the buds of his seven sacred centers have begun to unfold normally and enable him to contact and use the higher octaves of spiritual force so necessary to evolve his body to the point where he can enter the super-human kingdom, his ultimate destiny. But before he can reach this point man must learn to rule the animal desires and instincts and unfold the buds of his higher spiritual, as well as intellectual powers. For altho one may be a walking encyclopedia of facts and other men's ideas he cannot be considered truly intellectual until he has used his intellect to lead him upward to the next higher realm, that of spiritual consiousness

---

[9] *The Voice of Isis*, Curtiss, 244-316.

and realization of the Divine, both in the cosmos and within himself.

Because of the great and terrible dangers which could result from the premature development or misuse of the powers of these mystic centers, primitive man was warned by his Divine Instructors not to attempt to arouse or misuse the forces of these centers lest he surely die. For the consciousness of the undeveloped and spiritually unawakened—hence far more animal than spiritual—early Races naturally responded more strongly to the denser currents of force from the outer world than to the finer currents from the spiritual world. In gratifying their animal appetites they stimulated the lower creative centers far more than an ordinary animal would during normal procreation; for the animal is guided and controlled by instinct,[10] while man has free-will and is restrained from over-selfindulgence only by the influence of the indwelling Spiritual Man whose presence takes the place of instinct as the governing power. In other words, the early animal-man failed to discriminate in the use of his newly acquired self-consciousness and his physical senses. He therefore responded to the densest and most material aspects of the desires in which he found himself enveloped. These desires tempted him from following the Lord (Law), that is, the law that when instinct is superseded by self-consciousness all the creative powers must be guided and controlled by the higher consciousness of the Spiritual or Higher Self,

---

[10] For details see *The Voice of Isis*, Curtiss, 182.

instead of by the lower sense-consciousness of the animal in which the Higher Self is incarnated.

Since the human personality—the body plus as much of the Divine Consciousness as has been able to find even reflected if not direct expression—contains the Divine Spark, man inherits all the attributes and powers, at least potentially, of God his Father, one of the chief of which is the power to create at will, as well as to procreate as do the animals. It should be clearly understood that whenever used *the sex forces are always creative.*[11]

As we have already shown, all forms of creation take place in the subjective worlds—spiritual, mental or astral—even to the creation of a sonata, a play, a painting, a house or an automobile, and only later is the invisible creation or mental and astral pattern materialized or evolved on Earth thru the brain and hands of man, or in the case of Nature guided by the Creative Hierarchies working thru the elementals and nature sprites. But since the Divine Ideation creates only in harmony, beauty and perfection, it is the rebellious human personality, refusing to obey its Divine Guidance and to work in harmony with the Divine Law, and misusing its creative powers and the materials given it with which to evolve a perfect organism and environment for the use of its Divine Consciousness, that has created every form of inharmony, sin, sickness and disease, war, famine, pestilence and other disasters from which both the planet and man suffer.

---

[11] See The Voice of Isis, 218-19.

In fact, it is the sum total of these inharmonious worlds which constitutes what is known as hell and its devils.[12]

No wonder, then, in the Dark Ages when superstition flourished on ignorance of Nature's laws, that hell — and the devils (inharmonies) in man, which created it and kept it alive—was believed to be an eternal punishment for man! Yet already humanity is rapidly outgrowing that belief because the Divine Light of our Spiritual Consciousness is shining more and more deeply into the hells we have created, in order to illumine them and show us what they really are, and also to help us redeem them thru the radio-active power of the Divine Light.

Thus is good ultimately brought out of evil; not because "all is good" and there is good in evil, but because the Divine Law strives to bring the best possible results out of our mistakes and evil creations.[13] This is why all Souls who have evolved to the state where they must begin this redemptive process, either consciously or unconsciously, must descend into the hells of their creation, either through sickness, great sorrow, disaster or suffering of some kind, that through the strength and power of the Christ-force within, with which they meet these conditions and tests, they may conquer and prove their ability to take the still higher steps on the Path of Attainment. "If I ascend up into heaven, thou art there: if I make my bed in hell,

---

[12] See "The Doctrine of Hell Fire," *The Voice of Isis*, Curtiss, 75.

[13] "Human history has been guided more than we know; even national blunders have in the long run been overruled for good." Sir Oliver Lodge, *New York Times*, March 25, 1928, 13.

behold, thou art there. . . . Even there shall thy hand lead me, and thy right hand shall hold me. . . . Yea, the darkness hideth not from thee. . . . the darkness and the light are both alike to thee." By man came sin and death into the world and by man also must come the redemption. Only thus can hell be redeemed and its forces transmuted, for the individual and for the world. So clearly does Nature teach this lesson of redemption and the bringing of good out of evil that once it is pointed out to him, no thinking person can believe in eternal punishment or the supremacy of evil.

For generations theologians have reasoned from the false premise that because God is omnipotent, therefore He must have created all things. As a matter of fact, altho God is omnipotent, *He did not create all things*. But since we cannot conceive of God creating inharmony, evil, sin, disease and death, it is not necessary to assassinate our reason and disregard the evidence of all our senses and our experience in life by denying their existence, although this is an unwarranted conclusion to which certain mental science cults jump. All we need to do is to recognize that *there are two Creators*, a Greater and a lesser, God and His offspring, Man, who was created in His image and after His likeness, and who contains all His God-powers—including that of creating at will according to the thought held—and who, altho now but an apprentice, is destined some day to create even as his Father.

Therefore it was, not by the legitimate use of his

procreative power, but by the prostitution and perversion of all his creative powers—both mind and body and the misuse of the materials given him to fashion into a Garden of peace, purity and harmony—that man created such inharmony and impurity that he not only brought evil, sin, sickness and death upon himself, but also polluted the whole aura of Eden and cursed the very ground on which he walks.

It should be noted that the ground was not cursed by God—for we cannot imagine a God of Love and Justice, or any Divine Being cursing anything—but was cursed by the inharmonious, impure and perverted creations engendered, and still being engendered, by man himself. Even today virulent diseases arise spontaneously (endemically) in regions where they never occurred before and to which no source of infection can be traced, because the germs in the polluted astral world are precipitated into physical expression, by the Law of Manifestation already explained.

Throughout the past long cycles of evolution the hosts of evil, fashioned by man's thoughts and vitalized by his creative forces, have battled with the hosts of good, and this conflict has found its physical expression through many great wars, great epidemics, great catastrophes and cataclysms. But since all these results of man's inharmonious creation have not fully taught him his lesson, the accumulated evil still left unredeemed by his sacrifice and suffering is yet to be faced and overcome in the great Battle of Armageddon now being fought in the mental and astral worlds with thoughts and creative forces as weapons. And the results of this struggle between the ignorance, intolerance, hatred and impurity of mankind and his constructive and Godlike thoughts and creations, due to his response to the Divine Consciousness through thoughts of love, devotion, aspiration and unselfishness, must be precipitated upon the physical plane from which they arose and upon which they must find their final adjustment.[14]

Thank God that all man's thoughts and creations have not been evil! that one constructive, positive thought of good and helpfulness can neutralize and redeem many evil and destructive thoughts; that thousands upon thousands have sent out thoughts and prayers and have created plans for the betterment of mankind, so that the situation is far from being as hopeless as it looks; in fact, is distinctly encouraging. For every good thought is inspired by the divine side of man's consciousness, hence contains a higher creative potency and power, also is more enduring, altho finer and more subtle and hence more difficult of manifestation in dense Earth conditions. Moreover, every constructive and helpful thought, even if seemingly lost or smothered out by the hosts of evil, is gathered up, preserved and used by the warrior Angels as ammunition in the Battle of Armageddon.

As we have said elsewhere: The banishment of Adam and Eve from Eden was due to the fact that they could not face the Flaming Sword of Purity, which turned every way and barred them from obtaining the Fruit of the Tree of Life. This banishment

---

[14] See *Coming World Changes*, Curtiss, Chapter VI.

meant that man could no longer dwell in the etherealized body (Garden) with his spiritual faculties freely functioning and able to talk face to face with God.[15] This was not an instantaneous punishment, but took place thru the gradual separation of man's consciousness from that of the Higher Self, owing to man's greater materialization and his greater response to the sensations from the outer world. This gradual disuse of the function led to the atrophy of the organ of direct spiritual cognition (the *pineal gland*), whose reawakening and renewed functioning man must regain by conscious effort thru spiritual aspiration, prayer and endeavoring to let his life be governed by intuition and the Divine Law. Therefore, the true Soul or Real Self cannot fully dwell in the body of man as he is today, but can only project a Ray of Itself and endeavor to guide the human personality into the Path of Attainment and inspire him to seek the final At-one-ment.

While it was the destiny of both the globe and the incarnating Soul to manifest in the dense material conditions of our Earth, the vehicle or body built up of this physical material should have been kept so pure and sensitive that the Divine Self could have continued to dwell therein, instead of merely overshadowing it and incarnating only a Ray as at present. Only when the body is so purified that it can truly incarnate the Soul-consciousness, can we say with Jesus, "I and my Father are one."

---

[15] *The Voice of Isis*, Curtiss, 246-7.

CHAPTER XI

THE SERPENT POWER

> "Now the serpent was more subtle than any beast of the field which the Lord God had made. And he said onto the woman, Yea, hath God said, Ye shall not eat of every tree of the garden?... And the serpent said onto the woman, Ye shall not surely die: for God doth know that in the day ye eat thereof, then your eyes shall be opened; and ye shall be as gods, knowing good and evil." *Genesis*, III, 1-5.

The serpent was not the initiator of evil among mankind, but the initiator of wisdom; for the serpent was universally used among all ancient peoples as a symbol of Divine Wisdom.[1] Jesus referred to it in this sense when He admonished His disciples: "Be ye therefore wise as serpents and harmless as doves."[2] Assyrian and Druid priests were called Serpents of Wisdom, just as Initiates in India and Thibet today are called *Nagas* or Serpents.

To grow in size and expand it is necessary for a serpent to cast off its old, inelastic limiting skin at certain intervals. The serpent is therefore the universal symbol of that spiritual growth and expansion of consciousness by which alone Divine Wisdom can be attained. To advance spiritually we must cast off

---
[1] *Tree and Serpent Worship*, Furlong.
[2] *St. Matthew*, X, 16.

many misconceptions which, in our earlier stages of unfoldment, we thought were true spiritual teachings; yet true spiritual teachings are never a hampering skin, but bring inner illumination and expansion of consciousness. Therefore, by transcending the limitations of less mature conceptions, and by overcoming, transmuting or mastering the lower forces and temptations of "the world, the flesh and the devil," the Initiate is said to have cast off his outer hampering conditions as the serpent does his skin and to be "born again." In the *Bible* Moses is made to descend from the tribe of Levi, a serpent tribe. Gautama Buddha descended from a race of *Nagas* or Serpent Kings who ruled Magadha, and Hermes is represented by a snake symbol as Tet.[3]

The common misconception of the serpent symbol has created such a consciousness of evil that it is well to elaborate somewhat on its derivation and true meaning, according to Hebrew scholars who have specialized on the derivation of the word used.

"First, the word translated serpent is *not* the Hebrew word *Remes*, which means creeping things and reptiles. Second, at the time Moses wrote, the serpent was not the symbol of evil among any people in the world. The Hindoos regarded it as a symbol of *Life* and *reproductivity*. In Greece it was the *Protecting Genius* of the physician and *healing*. Among the Africans it was a symbol of *protecting good*; and

---

[3] For details see "Thy Symbol of the Serpent," *The Voice of Isis*, Curtiss, 241-55.

THE SERPENT POWER

in many other lands it was the symbol of *life* and *divine power of healing*. Third, among the Hebrews themselves, the serpent represented *God-power* from the time of Moses up to the time of Hezekiah. When Moses was still in Egypt he was commanded by the Lord God to cast his rod upon the ground; and when he did so, it became a serpent (*Exodus*, iv, 3.) This was a proof to Moses 'that God was *with* him.' When Moses wished to go before Pharaoh endowed with the *power of God*, he was commanded by the Lord God to carry with him the rod which could be turned into a serpent."[4]

It was using the word serpent in this sense of healing through a God-power that Moses was told to make a fiery serpent of brass and set it upon a pole or tree, by the beholding of which those who had been bitten by vipers would be healed. As a matter of fact, the Hebrew word (*Nachash*) translated *in this one instance* as serpent is the same word that is translated many times afterward as "brass." Seemingly, this translation of *Nachash* for serpent is an unbelievably careless or ignorant interpretation, *for it is the only place in the Bible* where it is translated as serpent. Only when the universal symbology of the serpent is understood is the translation seen to convey the idea intended, *i.e.*, Divine Wisdom.

Only since the Dark Ages, when the function of sex was condemned as evil by superficial students, has it been taught that the serpent symbolized the sex func-

---

[4] *The Four-fold Process of God Creation*, Landone, IV, 4.

tions. And it is still commonly so regarded today by the undiscriminating. But there is no warrant in the story of the Garden of Eden for any such assumption, for mere assumption it surely is.

According to the *Bible* story the sex function cannot be regarded as evil. It was built into man's body by the Creator himself. To think of the creative force as evil is to belittle the wisdom and goodness of God, who gave it to man, and attribute evil to Him. "If the so-called 'fall' occurred as a result of an act never intended by God or Nature and was a sin—how about the animals? Did they also sin in using their procreative powers?"[5] Manifestly such an idea is absurd. The misconception arises only through the speculations and misunderstandings of the philosophically unenlightened. For when God had created *all* things, "God saw *every* thing that he had made, and, behold, it was *very* good."[6] Hence, God made no mistake in providing man with that function, as many theological "wise men" think He did. Not only did God not make any mistake in providing the body with the sex function, but He picked out that function for particular commendation and *blessed it* and told man to use it normally for its proper use. "Be fruitful, and multiply, and replenish the earth, and subdue it."[7] "Shall mortal man be more just than God? Shall a man be more pure than his Maker?"[8] "What

---

[5] *The Secret Doctrine*, Blavatsky, II, 540.
[6] *Genesis*, I, 31.
[7] *Genesis*, I, 28.
[8] *Job*, IV, 17.

God hath cleansed, that call not thou common."[9]

As we have already said: If the Race is to be propagated in vileness, every child that is born must bear the burden of a thought of something vile and impure connected with its birth. It is no wonder that children so conceived have little love or respect for their unwilling parents. . . . For this reason the salvation of the Race depends upon the pure in heart conceiving children in love and purity, for if the perpetuation of the Race is left to the impure and ignorant, conditions must grow worse,[10] for this is one of the chief reasons for the large proportion of the unfit, from morons and the feeble-minded to the congenitally insane.

Since the use of this function is the only method by which an immortal Soul or Spiritual Being can find incarnation on Earth, and since it was the only function man was specifically told to use, and whose use was specifically blessed, it certainly is not evil in itself, nor was its use prohibited. All such ideas have arisen from misconceptions of it due to a materialistic and unenlightened medieval interpretation of the allegory.

As we have already explained: This belief has given rise to doctrines which teach man to despise and try to kill out this greatest of gifts. But as long as this serpent of sex is accursed and degraded by man's thought, it is doomed to crawl upon the ground and bring forth its progeny of vipers in darkness and filth, and woman is doomed to conceive and bring forth in

---

[9] *Acts*, X, 15.
[10] *The Voice of Isis*, 225-6.

pain and suffering instead of Purity and Joy. Woman has suffered the most, but by that suffering she should have developed her spiritual intuition.[11]

The sex-force is considered impure only because the spiritually blind have decreed that it shall be considered impure. They assume that they are wiser and holier than He who created them, He who breathed into them the Living Fire of creative force. Being wiser than the gods, they have decreed that the normal expression of the sex-function (even within the married relation) shall be considered vile and that it shall be suppressed. The result is already apparent.[11]

What then is the true meaning of the word translated "serpent"? And what the meaning of the allegory as a whole? The Hebrew word used is *Nachash*, whose root meaning is "divine experience." The serpent is represented as "beguiling" Eve. The word translated as "beguiled" is *Nasha*, whose root meaning is "to lift up" "*Nasha*, the form used in the verse under discussion, is translated as *lifted up* in the text of the *Standard Protestant Concordance*. . . . *It is never mis-translated beguiled in any other place in the Bible*."[12] Therefore, what Eve really said was that, because she followed what Divine Wisdom (serpent) told her, a "divine experience" had lifted her up, and she naturally wished Adam to share it with her. What was this divine experience? *It was certainly not the*

---

[11] *The Voice of Isis*, Curiss, 249-50.
[12] *The Four-fold Process of God Creation*, Landone, IV, 4.

use of the sex function, for it was not until far later, after they had left Eden (iv, i), that "Adam knew Eve his wife; and she conceived, and bare Cain."

This explanation of the symbology of Eve and the serpent confirms what we said in Chapter VIII as to the role woman was meant to play. Being the more intuitive of the twain who are one, she has the gift of being able to see and understand the mystical truths and ideals of the serpent (Divine Wisdom) necessary for both. And she is not fulfilling her mission unless she presents them for man to share.

The experience of so-called temptation is correctly described as being due to a serpent because it referred to the serpentine character of that mysterious force for which we have no term in English, but which in the Sanskrit is called the *kundalini-force*. The development and use of this force in the unfolding of the psychic centers of the body is as highly technical a science as is the use of electricity, the X-rays, or radium, and about which little of its practical functioning is known in the Western world, but concerning which many ponderous volumes have been written.[13] And it is even more dangerous if attempted without the personal training and oversight of one who—as in the other sciences mentioned above—is thoroughly versed in its laws and is an adept in its use. We can, therefore, refer to it here only in general outline, just suf-

---

[13] For pictures of the centres and diagrams of the current pathways see *The Serpent Power*, Avalon, Madras; *Fundamental Principles of Operative Occultism*, Hall; *The Encricled Serpent*, Howey, etc.

ficient to meaning of the tree, the serpent and the temptation. Basically it is "an electrospiritual force, a creative power which, when aroused into action, can as easily kill as it can create."[14] Just so with the creative power of sex. It can be used normally both to provide bodies for the Souls who are seeking incarnation on Earth, and also as an expression of affection and love which shall unite the twain as one with that Divine Love which is their Source. But if the sex functions are concentrated upon and artificially stimulated and worshipped from babyhood for the purpose of ministering merely to an abnormally stimulated lust,[15] then it brings forth only the weeds of the Garden—physical degeneration and moral degradation, sin, loathsome diseases and premature death.

Since brass is an alloy composed of two metals, copper (belonging to Venus, Divine Love) and zinc (connected with the Earth), its composition symbolizes that for the proper manifestation of the serpent on Earth there must be an alloy or combination of its two elements, the heavenly and the earthly; Divine Wisdom and the physical *kundalini-force* lifted up to the pole of the spinal cord, or the sap of the "tree."

In the average man the serpent-power normally passes around and up the spinal cord—the "tree" in the midst of the Garden (body)—reflexly and without man's being aware of it, in a spiral or serpentine manner. Its positive and negative currents are called

---

[14] The *Voice of the Silence*, Blavatsky, note to page 7.
[15] For details see *Mother India*, Mayo.

Ida and *Pingalla*, and they cross over each other at certain levels to form nodes of force or chakras. This is all graphically outpictured in the *Caduceus* or Wand of Hermes, the use of which is said to confer both healing and wisdom. This symbol consists of a straight rod, representing the spinal cord, surmounted by a knob, representing the *medulla oblongata* and the head, with two serpents twining around the rod from bottom to top. It is used today as the symbol of the physician.

When properly unfolded, controlled and used uprightly this serpent-power no longer twines around the spinal cord like a serpent, but passes directly up the central canal of the spinal cord to the brain, changing from a serpent into a rod of power, the God-power symbolized by the Rod of Moses and Aaron, the Wand of Hermes, and the *Brahmadanda* or knotted stick carried by Hindu ascetics. For there comes a time in the spiritual unfoldment of every Soul when the spiritual seed of Christhood, planted in the Garden of man's physical body at the base of the spine, begins to put forth. Then the manifestation of this spiritual fire, this spiritual creative force, like a mighty volcano, begins to erupt; for it must push its way upward through all obstacles and make straight the path of God-consciousness, instead of following the serpentine path as during the less developed stages of spiritual evolution or when used for mere psychic development.

During the process of making a straight path to the brain the ascending *kundalini-fire* or serpent-power stimulates into a higher octave of activity the seven sacred centers or chakras along the spine whose higher functioning gives to man the *sidis* or super-physical psychic powers. These are not spiritual powers in themselves, for their development merely enables man to use his five senses in a higher octave of vibration or function consciously in that semi-physical world which is just above the physical world.[16] But when this current of spiritual fire reaches the brain it stimulates those higher centers whose unfoldment brings to man that "divine experience" or spiritual illumination promised to Eve by the serpent, by means of which man should become "as gods, knowing good and evil" and whose proper use will ultimately enable man to face the Flaming Sword and re-enter Eden from which the Law of Good (Lord God) drove him when he had ignorantly aroused and perverted the serpent-power.

As the serpent-force spreads out at the base of the brain and then pushes upward to the top of the head it forms a small cross called the "cross of suffering." For it is upon this cross that the body is crucified as the atoms of the flesh are subjected to the transmuting and spiritualizing effects of this spiritual fire. It is this mystic cross which forms the hilt of the Sword of the Spirit and is symbolized by the cross on the hilt of the swords of the Knights of the Holy Grail whose real, mystic quest was none other than the attainment of this same "divine experience" of spiritual illumination.

---

[16] See *Realms of the Living Dead*, Curtiss, 201-4.

When aroused artificially and without proper preparation or out of due season, or if improperly controlled and perverted, the serpent-power stimulates only the lower aspects of the centers and thus tempts man to use his newly discovered creative powers of mind and body for self-gratification and the self-indulgence of the merely animal nature, so that sex impulses are often mistaken for desires of the Real Self. This brings about an entirely different kind of crucifixion: not the voluntary crucifixion of spiritualization and transmutation which enables man to enter the next higher kingdom of Super-man, but the involuntary crucifixion of the flesh—through disease and degeneration—which sinks man below the level of the animal kingdom beneath him.

CHAPTER XII

THE SERPENT POWER (Concluded)

> "Thou shalt surely die is usually considered a penalty for man's defilement of Eden, but in reality even this death sentence was but the working of the immutable Law of Divine Love; for immortality under conditions of imparity, sickness and suffering, would be a punishment for surpassing even the medieval conceptions of a physical hell." *The Voice of Isis*, Curtiss, 247.

In the early Races when the forces of evolution were focused on the body and on the development of the newly acquired fifth principle, self-conscious mind, the stimulus of the *kundalini* was so great that its vibrations very largely shut out those of the Inner Guidance. That is, the more the attention was occupied by the vibrations of mind and of the outside world, the less attention was given to the inner spiritual vibrations from the Real Self, just as is the case today. It was, therefore, this mind, which should have ruled the Garden as a husbandman under the direction of the Lord God, which was perverted by the vibrations of the desires of the flesh and the things of the outer world.

It was because of this misuse of the serpent-power that the serpent is represented as being cursed. "Upon thy belly shalt thou go, and dust shalt thou eat all the days of thy life."[1] For just as the Rod of Moses and Aaron became a serpent when cast upon the ground, so does the *kundalini-fire* become a stinging serpent when allowed to crawl upon the ground instead of being lifted up into a Rod of Power. As long as man's creative power is allowed to crawl upon its belly it must eat of the dust or the offscourings of the Earth, and bring to man the dire results which curse him,[2] "visiting the iniquity of the fathers upon the children, and upon the children's children, unto the third and to the fourth generation."[3] We must remember that neither the ground nor the serpent-power was cursed by God, but was cursed by the evil which resulted from man's misuse and perversion of his creative powers of body and mind. Only as man lifts up the serpent-power upon the pole or "tree" (spinal cord) in the wilderness of the outer life, as Moses lifted it up on a pole in the wilderness—*i.e.*, lives a life of purity, chastity and wise control—can it become the God-power which shall restore to health all man's functions and faculties (symbolized by the children of Israel) which have been poisoned by the vipers of impurity and perversion.

In this sense the serpent symbolizes humanity as a whole; for as long as humanity "crawls upon its belly" or does not lift its consciousness up from crawling on the physical plane and following after appe-

---

[1] *Genesis*, III, 14.
[2] See *Mother India*, Mayo.
[3] *Exodus*, XXXIV, 7.

tites, desires and lusts of the belly, and does not seek for spiritual food, it must expect to reap, in suffering and sorrow, the results of feeding upon the offscourings or dust of the ground as well as the dust of ignorance and old conceptions long since proved to be but the dust of the ages. As long as he crawls upon his belly man is in very truth a stinging serpent, poisoning his own life, his fellowmen and society as a whole. But with his creative powers of mind and body uplifted by a determined will as strong and shining as brass, and illumined by the celestial light that shines from his at-one-ment with the Lord God or Law of his Good, the radio-activity of the spiritual God-power flowing through him will help to heal all those who are bitten by the vipers of sin, sickness and sorrow; for, to everyone who looks to him and recognizes the brazen will or illumined serpent-power, he will bring life and healing.

If, therefore, the "fruit of the tree" is eaten ere it is ripe, that is, if man attempts to use these higher mystic powers ere he has reached the stage of spiritual growth and gained the spiritual understanding through which alone he can normally unfold these centers like the petals of a rose, the attempt to use them can bring only inharmony, suffering and premature death. Far better not eat of the fruit of these higher powers at all, that is, it is far better to be just a good, wholesome, normal human being and take a little longer to evolve into the Super-human kingdom, than to try to force a development for which neither mind, character nor body is normally prepared.

When man is unprepared for its proper control and use, the very God-power, or the divine ecstasy of the serpent-power itself, which is given to man in due season to make him as the gods, "knowing good and evil," becomes the Flaming Sword which guards the gates—centers or chakras—of the Garden. For ere man can safely use the super-normal God-powers in such a way that *Nachash*, the "divine experience" can "beguile" or "lift him up" into the ecstasy of spiritual consciousness, he must have gained the wisdom and the moral strength of character to use such higher dynamic powers *consciously*, and *constructively*, under the guidance of the Lord God of his Garden, or the Indwelling Spiritual Man or Higher Self within.

To every Soul who sincerely strives to do his best, according to his stage of evolution, to express harmony in his life and helpfulness to his fellowman, the time will come in some incarnation when these centers will open as normally as the petals of a rose. But if he tries to force them open ere they are ready, the beauty and fragrance and joy of life will wither and fall to the ground and be lost in the dust of the earth like fallen petals.

It is usually understood that Adam and Eve were driven out of their Garden for having used the perfectly natural and normal functions of sex. But we are distinctly told (Genesis, iii, 22-3) that *this was not the reason*. They were banished from the Garden lest they partake of that other Tree, the Tree of Life, and become immortal and live forever in the flesh. "Behold, the man is become as one of us, to know good and evil: and now, lest he put forth his hand; and take also of the tree of life, and eat, and live forever: *therefore* the Lord God sent him forth from the garden of Eden." For to attain immortality in the flesh while still enveloped in a grossly animal body as defective and unevolved as it was during the early Races, or even in the more evolved body of man today, which is still such a hampering garment for the expression of the indwelling Spiritual Man, would be a greater curse than any imaginable hell.

Man was first turned out of his Garden individually not by God but by his own misuse of his opportunities, forces and materials which brought death, with all its attendant ills and miseries, first into his own body and then into the body politic. Thus man finds death mixed with every draught of life, and his Eden no longer a pure and perfect globe, but impregnated with death; and his body no longer a quiet protected Garden filled with goodly fruits which are his for the picking; for by his actions he has automatically turned himself out of the Garden lest he eat of the Tree of Life and live forever in imperfection.

Since inharmony, sin, sickness and death cannot exist in the pure aura of the Real or Spiritual Self, the sinful man had to be cast out of his Garden where all things are pure, perfect and immortal, and where health and happiness are his natural heritage. Man can re-enter his Garden only when he has so purified himself in mind and body that his vibrations are so greatly raised as once more to coincide with those of the Garden. But, once man was precipitated out of the Garden, thenceforth he must till the soil of earth conditions from the outside "by the sweat of his brow"; must learn through physical exertion, experience and suffering that these conditions are not his real home; must learn to recognize the sphere of Divine Consciousness and radiant spiritual force which is his true home or Garden, and seek to prepare himself to re-enter it in a spiritual and immortalized body.

Only when man has learned that mind is but a gift of God to be used for His glory; that illumined spiritual consciousness can be bestowed upon him only by a Power outside of and above mind—through spiritual development and initiation into a higher stage of consciousness—can he return to his Garden. Only when we learn that mind is merely the servant of the Real Self or the superintendent of our Garden unto whom is given the wise direction of all its forces, yet who must be responsible to the Lord of Life who is the real Indweller, can the serpent be turned into the Rod of Power at whose knock the gates of Eden shall fly open and admit us to our heritage.[4]

---

[4] The *Message of Aquaria*, Curtiss, 397.

CHAPTER XIII

UNITY IN DUALITY

"Love is self-completion by the union of corresponding opposites in the same substance, and Sex has its origin in the very nature of Deity." *The Perfect Way*, Kingsford, 58.

"The underlying reality which finds ultimate expression in the physical bodies of individuals, is the principle of the positive and negative forces of the Universal Life Energy, which has brought all organised forms into existence, from the compounds of mineral atoms to man." *The Seventh Seal*, Agnes, 80.

If we study the book of Nature as a primer in which the Law of Manifestation is shown worked out for us in the lower kingdoms, we find that all things have their beginning in some kind of germ or tiny seed, some little and seemingly insignificant happening, often very remote from the results, just as an entire city may be devastated by a fire which sprang from a tiny spark carelessly dropped miles away or by a tidal wave resulting from an upheaval in a far-distant ocean. The city is not destroyed as a punishment, but as the outworking of inexorable laws, both physical and karmic. Hence it is the seed-cause which we must find and counteract if we are to change the results. For karmic conditions which may devastate a region, a nation or a Race, may arise from just such seemingly insignificant and remote causes. It is a lack of understanding of such causes—which results from a lack of proper moral and religious instruction—that is causing many thousands today to say: "Let us eat, drink and be merry, for tomorrow we die."

One of the fundamental laws of Nature which strikes to the very heart of civilization and all organized society is the Law of Sex.[1] And here we must remind our readers of what we have repeatedly stated elsewhere,[2] namely, that this Earth is a planet purposely created as a stage upon which is to be worked out a new scene in the great cosmic drama, a new problem and test not found on any other planet, *i.e.*, the problem of the manifestation of the spiritual unity of the Soul in the duality of the sexes. Hence the Law of Sex, and all that pertains to it, is the lesson of lessons for mankind to learn, all others being secondary and relative. Our failure to learn this lesson, and the consequent misuse and perversion of our creative forces, is the underlying cause of the troubles and disasters of all kinds which we are now reaping,[3] not as a punishment, but so to awaken man to his dependence upon the Divine and his need for seeking out and obeying the Divine Law that his mind can be illuminated to understand and correct his mistakes or else pass out of physical incarnation and learn the lesson in the higher realms.

---

[1] See *The Key to the Universe*, Curtiss, 87.
[2] See *The Voice of Isis*, Curtiss, 46.
[3] See *Coming World Changes*, Curtiss.

This is the mighty Law which, altho known from the beginning to the Initiates and their advanced disciples, is only now beginning to be recognized and appreciated in its true light by the enlightened students of human progress. But humanity will pay attention and follow this Law only when at least a nucleus of enlightened Souls are willing to devote thought and attention and the example of their lives to the promulgation of the fundamental spiritual principles underlying this question, and thus take it out of the realm of mere animal self-indulgence.

Just as surely as this planet is one expression or an outbreathing of that God-consciousness which underlies, enfolds and sustains it, thru the interaction of its positive and negative aspects, just so surely is the Soul of a man a Ray of that same God-consciousness striving to manifest its Divinity thru two separated bodies of flesh. These bodies, being of the earth earthy, naturally obscure and limit the outshining of the immortal Soul-consciousness according to the degree of their density and lack of response to their Divine Guidance. But these bodies are nevertheless absolutely necessary as instruments by and thru which the Soul can contact and find expression in the world of matter. Hence they are neither to be despised nor their functions belittled, killed out or perverted. Since they are composed of the same substances as the Earth, gathered together and built up by Inner Pattern, these bodies must follow the laws of physical evolution, "under severe penalty of abnormal growth, with all its ensuing results."

Since the body is but the Soul's instrument of manifestation, chief importance should be given to Soul qualities and spiritual principles, instead of to the mental and bodily functions thru which these Soul qualities and spiritual principles must necessarily find expression. And it is only thru Divine Guidance, illumination and spiritual realization, and thru divinely inspired teachings—not thru mere intellectual activity and reason—that the eternal verities and spiritual ideals can be apprehended. But once these ideals are "spiritually discerned" and presented to the mind, then thought and reason are responsible for their outworking and manifestation. Unless we understand the *spiritual basis and ideals* of sex, the mind and reason can easily be led astray into self-indulgence and animalism by all sorts of sophistries which appear sound and reasonable until checked up and weighed by the true spiritual ideals or else by the inevitable suffering which results from following such sophistries.

As we have explained elsewhere: Man is the masculine Ray or the expression on Earth of the Divine Father-force, that aspect of the Divine which is ever fructifying, ever creating and expressing itself in forms. It is a personalization of that Divine Potency designated in the Creed as, "God, Father Almighty, maker of all things visible and invisible." Hence, since man expresses this Father-ray, he is the positive pole and his function in life is creativeness. Therefore, the foundation of all his love and his seeking for union with God expresses itself in the desire to fructify and create. Woman, on the other hand, is the expression of the divine Mother-force, that which is called the "Holy Ghost," the "Comforter"; in Egyptian symbology, Isis the Great Mother, and in Hindu philosophy, Vishnu the preserver. Hence the foundation of all woman's love is divine Motherhood.[4]

The expression of Mother-love is woman's nearest approach to the divine state; therefore, the more a woman loves, the more the element of mothering, even her husband, enters into it. Even though she have no children she will mother all she loves, for this is the fundamental wellspring of her very existence as a separated sex. For this reason we often find that a woman can live in happiness and express her love in caresses, cherishing and in motherly solicitude. But a man has his equally strong and divine love built upon the great Father-force of creativeness, hence the more true, sincere and Godlike man grows, the higher, purer and more intense will be his desire to fructify and create on all planes. If these two great and fundamental laws of the opposite poles of sex-life were better understood there would not only be less marital unhappiness, but the Race as a whole would evolve much more quickly back to its Edenic oneness.[4]

The great lesson for each to learn is that the functions of sex are Divine and are not a gift given to man and woman as evolved animal organisms merely

---

[4] See *The Key to the Universe*, Curtiss, 88-9.

for the purpose of procreation and peopling the Earth, but are innate God-qualities, *the very essence of their divine oneness* which they as immortal Souls must manifest thru their animal bodies. This is necessary as a means of informing, purifying and evolving those animal bodies to a state of perfection in which the complete God-consciousness can flow unimpeded from one to the other, and they can be as truly one on Earth in two separated bodies as they were in the higher worlds, yet with all the experience gained from the long journey into the far country of embodiment, and the strength and power of son-hood which has made them truly "as one of us," the Elohim.[4]

We see, therefore, that sex in man is not merely an animal function, for the purpose of propagation of the species, but inheres in the Soul itself as the Great Creative Force given it by the Father, and exceeds the mere procreative powers of the animal to at least as great a degree as the Soul of man exceeds the animal. For it is one avenue for the expression of the spiritually creative power of the incarnating Spirit or "Living Soul" which inhabits the human animal body. With it, after many experiences in building up physical instruments in many incarnations, man must at last learn how to create a perfect Temple of the Living God. "Know ye not that ye are the temple of God, and that the Spirit of God dwelleth in you? If any man defile the temple of God him shall God destroy: for the temple of God is holy, *which temple ye are*."[5]

---

[5] *I Corinthians*, III, 16, 17.

The bodily organs, therefore, are but the specialized avenues for the expression of the positive and negative creative aspects of the Soul. And their activity is as pure, natural and normal as the activity of the heart and lungs. We do not call thought a "mere animal function" because it has a physical organ (the brain) thru which it functions, even tho it can function for the grossest animal ends as well as for the highest ideals. No more, then, should we say that sex is "merely an animal function" because it has physical organs thru which it manifests physically; for, altho they can be used for the grossest animal indulgence, they can also be used to induce the greatest spiritual ecstasy. "That which is called sex when operating thru the sex organs of the body, becomes Divine Creative Force when operating thru Nature; Creative Ideation when functioning thru the mind, and the outgoing of the Divine Breath, or the Urge to Manifest, of the God-creativeness, when functioning thru the Cosmos."[6]

The oneness of the two, or Unity in Duality, we have seen is illustrated by the allegory of Eve being taken from Adam's side and by the tree in the midst of the Garden of Eden, which was a symbol of the great and primary lesson of sex, *i.e.*, the oneness of the two who spiritually belong to each other, the one representing the leaves, the other the seed-bearer or fruit, yet both the expressions of the one sap. And only as man learns this lesson and makes it govern his

---

[6] *The Key to the Universe*, Curtiss, 34.

whole life, can he attain true peace, harmony and love on Earth and co-operate with the Divine as a perfect instrument for His manifestation on Earth.

Only as he eats of the fruit of the Tree of Good and Evil in accordance with the Divine Law will it prove good and make him "as the gods," for it will produce endless evil when partaken of merely as an animal function and with any but his true spiritual mate.[7] Like the tree, there must be the outer framework, the branches and the leaves—the masculine elements—which are able to withstand the storms and stresses of physical conditions, yet these alone can never form a perfect tree. There must also be the inner sap which draws from the earth, the air, the water and the Sun the inner life-essences with which to vitalize the outer form and bring forth beauteous blossoms and nourishing fruit—the feminine elements. Therefore, only as man and woman learn this lesson of oneness, harmony and perfect co-operation on all planes can they enter into a true understanding of their life on Earth and a realization of their immortal Destiny.

---

[7] For the proof of the doctrine of spiritual mates see *The Key to the Universe*, Curtiss, Chapters, IX, XII; *The Seventh Seal*, Agnes; *The Harmonics of Evolution*, Huntley; *The Dream Child*, Huntley.

CHAPTER XIV

THE TWAIN ONE FLESH

"But *from the beginning* of the creation God made them male and female. For this cause shall a man leave his father and mother and cleave to his wife; and they twain shall be one flesh: so then *they are no more twain, but one flesh*. What therefore *God* hath joined together, let not man put asunder." *St. Mark*, X, 6-9.

"All Souls are pre-existent in the world of emanations, and are in their original estate androgynous, but when they descend upon the earth they become separated into male and female, and inhabit different bodies; if therefore in this life the male half encounters the female half, a strong attachment springs up between them, and hence it be said that in marriage the separated halves are again conjoined; and. . . . are akin to the Kerubim." *The Kabbalah Unveiled*, Mathers, 34-5.

In a previous volume we have shown that: All manifestations of the Godhead must contain a reflection of the triangle—(a) the inner reality, (b) the outer manifestation, and (c) the life-force which unites the two—else the Deity would not be represented in His works.[1] In this volume we have shown that as the androgynous Soul, the Spiritual Man or Higher Self, descends into this world of material manifestation and comes under the overruling Law of Duality, the Soul must separate into its masculine and feminine expressions, man and woman. Since these

---
[1] *The Key to the Universe*, Curtiss, 106.

two separated Rays of the Divine proceed from the same Divine Source they can find the perfect expression of their divinity on Earth only as they find each other and unite to form the base line of the perfectly balanced equilateral triangle whose apex is their Higher Self or the personal Father-in-heaven common to both. Herein we have plainly pointed out that true marriage is really made in heaven where the two are one before their separation on the physical plane. We have also presented the diagrams[2] which give the geometrical proof that a true marriage cannot take place between *any* man and *any* woman, but only between one particular man and one particular woman, namely, the particular individuals who embody the masculine and feminine Rays from the same Soul or Higher Self.

This, of course, is no new doctrine, but has been taught throughout the ages by the great philosophers and spiritual teachers of practically every age and every race. Jesus plainly taught this when He said: "*From the beginning* of the creation God made them male and female. . . . What therefore God hath joined together, let not man put asunder."[3] Only the two who are manifestations of the one androgynous Soul or Higher Self and who are already one in the higher realms "from the beginning of the creation" are the ones whom God hath joined together, and not *any* man and *any* woman; for it could only be the

---

[2] The Key to the Universe, Curtiss, 109-110.
[3] *St Mark*, X, 2-9.

particular man and the *particular* woman who were true complementary spiritual mates who were joined "from the beginning of the creation." These are the ones who may not be put asunder.

In the above quotation Jesus had just approved of divorce for those whom God had not joined. Hence He implied that no mere human ceremony could constitute a true spiritual marriage, for a human ceremony cannot join the two "from the beginning of the creation." It can only give public recognition to and solemnize the union on Earth of the particular two whom God hath already joined in the higher realms from the beginning.

The fact that we may feel strongly drawn to several persons of the opposite sex is not an argument against the fact that there is but one in particular who is our mate. It simply means that all such are persons with whom we have set up strong ties in past lives; ties of brother and sister, parent and child, friendship, business, personal service, or of man and wife, even when not mates. When we meet such persons in this life we naturally feel the vibration of the old attraction—or perhaps antipathy. This attraction is often mistaken for that of the true mate, but marriages made under such conditions can never be satisfactory. Those who desire promiscuity in this life are those who have been promiscuous in past lives and have not yet learned their lesson, hence will have to go thru the resulting suffering again in this life.

As we have previously explained: If, for instance,

a masculine personality or expression of the Higher Self A unites with the feminine expression of the same Higher Self A—to which it could alone truly belong—as they advance spiritually and evolve upward toward the Higher Self common to both they must necessarily grow closer to each other on all planes (see diagram)[4] for they are evolving toward union with the same overshadowing Higher Self. But if a positive personality of the Higher Self A should unite with a negative personality of the Higher Self of which it is not an emanation—say of the Higher Selves B or C—then as each personality advanced spiritually and evolved upward along its Ray toward union with its Higher Self, instead of the two personalities growing closer together on all planes, they must inevitably grow farther and farther apart on the higher planes—and this must ultimately lead to separation on the physical plane—for each one is evolving toward union with a different Higher Self.[4]

Therefore, there may develop great inharmony on the physical plane in this case, not because they are becoming less spiritual, but because they are advancing and being drawn into different currents of force which do not harmonize or lead to the same Higher Self. And as the great Law of Divine Love ever seeks greater and more perfect expressions of harmony, the Great Law tends to separate them that each may be able to manifest a higher state of harmony. In such

---

[4] *The Key to the Universe*, Curtiss, 109-110.

cases separation[4] on the physical plane, instead of being a calamity, is a blessing and an absolute necessity for the spiritual advance of each.[5]

Since the masculine and feminine aspects of the Soul were necessarily separated to enable them to incarnate in the flesh, naturally the ideal state when thus incarnated is for the two to be united on Earth—as they already are in heaven—in the exclusive and God-ordained marriage relation. *The highest ideal of the evolution of the Soul in matter is, therefore, the reunion of the separated aspects of the Soul, and their learning, hand in hand, the great lessons for which the Soul comes to Earth.*

Unless the marriage relation contained a function, an experience and a lesson necessary for the Soul's perfect unfoldment, the all-wise and loving Creator would never have made such a function a fundamental law of man's existence: even of Nature itself. No one, therefore, who advocates celibacy or the killing out of this function as the ideal, can possibly fulfill the Law of Duality thereby. But we must have an adequate conception of the problem and study its ideals, as revealed through inspiration from the higher realms, if we are to understand how properly to fulfill the Law.

Thru this study we see that the Law is fulfilled only thru Love; for Love, which is God, is the fulfilling of

---

[4] See footnote, page 153.
[5] See Chapter on "Marriage and Divorce" in *Letters from the Teacher*, II, Curtiss.

the Law, or that purifying, spiritualizing, and transmuting Divine Radiation which, when truly invoked, raises the function far above its mere physical aspect of animal gratification and procreation to a spiritual union of Soul with Soul. While the outer man is an animal he is capable of grasping that which is more than animal; for the presence of the Inner Man made in the Image of God enables man to raise his conception of the marriage relation from a mere animal function to that of a sacred sacrament in which the physical relation and its sensations are transcended and the separated personalities are temporarily merged into the one Spiritual Essence, the Soul, so that the twain become one flesh, altho in separated bodies.

Sexual union merely for the satisfaction of animal-passion between any but true mates is a union of body only and not of Soul. And as their polarities are not complementary on all planes, even if they are so on the physical, such a union cannot make the magnetic conditions so necessary for the inflow of the higher spiritual currents which produce the spiritual and re-generative effects. Such a union, therefore, creates only after the lusts of the flesh, for the true love and aspiration so necessary to generate the spiritual impulse which draws down the Divine Fire—also necessary to generate children of the New Age—is lacking; in fact is impossible under such conditions.

Therefore, there can never be true satisfaction, even physically—only temporary animal gratification—between the unmated or thru promiscuous intercourse.

If the two are not spiritual mates the union can never bring the perfect satisfaction, harmony and happiness of Unity in Duality. For there can be no true satisfaction on Earth except as the human personality makes contact with and temporarily expresses a vibration from the Spiritual or Higher Self, from the thrill that results from an unselfish deed, a kind word or a generous forgiveness, to the ecstasy of conscious union between true mates with their common Higher Self. In the union of such mates, altho animal gratification is not the object or the thought held, the animal nature is more than satisfied, purely incidentally, for it is engulfed in and uplifted and its consciousness transcended by the vibrations of unity with the Divine which such a union produces. Also in such a union there are no psychological obstructions to the inflow of the higher currents, for there is no sense of shame, guilt or impurity to short-circuit such currents; only an overflowing and all-encompassing realization of Divine Love.

In this connection we often hear remarks from so called advanced women students that they have "risen above" or have "outgrown" or "advanced beyond" all sex desires. Such expressions show a total misconception of the entire subject which is the natural outcome of the false interpretations of the doctrines of the "fall of man" and "original sin"; of something inherently impure in the sex relation. When such statements are sincere and not the result of self-righteousness and a desire of the woman to appear superior to her husband, it shows that her attitude of mind—her attitude of non-co-operation or even aversion—has so short-circuited both the higher spiritual currents, and even the physical magnetic currents, that she has become frigid and incapable of response. She thus makes the ceremony as unsatisfactory to her husband as to herself.

Through the results of her misunderstanding of this function and her mistaken attitude of mind concerning it she has only too often added to the already great army of unhappy and ineffectual marriages which are a great factor in holding back the higher unfoldment of mankind. And inharmony, suffering and disease are the result on Earth, while in the higher realms the great army of advanced Souls who are seeking the conditions of understanding, peace, harmony and love so necessary for their incarnation are crying out, "How long, O Lord? How long?"

To think of the sex relation as a weakness of the flesh which should not be yielded to is a perversion of both mind and a God-given function. For without the right attitude of mind the mere union of the bodies cannot produce that magnetic and vibratory harmony—physically, mentally and spiritually—which alone can bring down into the body the uplifting and transforming effects of the Spirit or which can give incarnation to advanced sensitive Souls.

No woman who is normal physically can be frigid unless she short-circuits herself by her mental attitude. If she desires to respond and cannot do so there is something abnormal, some physical disability—some contraction, adhesion, misplacement or tumor, etc.—which can usually be easily remedied by her family physician. All such conditions are physical results built into the body because of false conceptions of sex in this and past incarnations: of believing that God made sex as a temptation to be overcome or as but a degrading animal function that He was unable to eliminate when He created man in His own image and likeness. We have shown in previous chapters that sex can never be wiped out or done away with as long as man manifests on Earth under the Law of Duality. But it can and must be purified of the false conceptions in regard to it and used for its highest ends. Nor can sin, sickness and disease be overcome and its further generation stopped until humanity has learned this lesson; for these things can never be driven from the Earth as long as mankind continues to create them thru the ignorant and perverted use of his creative powers, due to lack of proper instruction and wrong thought concerning them.

If a wife is really more "advanced" and more spiritually unfolded than her husband, instead of self-frighteously looking down upon him as a mere male with unspiritualized animal instincts which must be indulged under protest, she should be the one to lift his mind above mere animal instincts and teach him to hold the right thought: the thought that the marriage rite involves something far higher than unlimited gratification of animal passion. She may look upon sex as a mere animal function, but what animal does not use it normally? or what animal ever perverts it into the horrible orgies of lust which some persons make of it because of a lack of such understanding, teaching and control as the truly "advanced" woman should teach her husband? "What God hath cleansed, that call not thou common" might better read, "What God hath cleansed, that make ye not common and un-clean." "For this is the will of God, even your sanctification. . . . that every one of you should know how to possess his vessel [body] in sanctification and honour; not in the lust of concupiscence. . . . For God hath not called us unto uncleanness, but unto holiness. He therefore that despiseth, despiseth not man, but God."[6]

While response of the body is necessary so that even the body may ultimately awaken in the Image of God, nevertheless that response is neither the aim nor the end of the union. The ideal to be held by both is that the physical union merely completes on the physical plane the union of the two aspects of the Soul which are one in the higher realms. For we should understand that the body has been evolved thus far not merely as a physical covering for the Soul, but must continue to evolve until it literally expresses the beauty of holiness of the Divine Indweller. We must so sanctify all our acts and thoughts that our whole body shall be full of light.

The union on all planes can be accomplished only

---

[6] *I Thessalonians*, IV, 3-7.

thru love; that quality of love which, while not ignoring the physical aspect, yet far transcends it; that quality of love which can exist only between one particular man and one particular woman who are true spiritual complements or mates. Only such can form a magnet which shall draw down the Divine Fire from heaven to sanctify their union and consume all dross of sensuality. In other words, there must be no thought or impulse that can act as a barrier between the twain and the consciousness of the presence of God-love manifesting between and thru them. Until this higher consciousness exists, the ideal conditions have not been attained.

Real marriage is, therefore, truly made in heaven, and its proper consummation on Earth brings that heavenly consciousness down to Earth to the extent of its realization. And this comes about only thru pure love and mutual aspiration for union with the Divine and not merely thru a union of the sexes. Such truly mated Souls whom God hath joined from the beginning no man can put asunder. It is only the man-made marriages not made in heaven or of the Soul—not made in response to the inner Soul-guidance, but for all sorts of worldly reasons and the mere lusts of the flesh—that can and should be put asunder, for they are not married in the sight of God, hence naturally fall asunder. For nothing can constitute a true marriage save the call of Divine Love for union of the separated aspects of the same Soul. This is the Divine Urge ever working to manifest the Law of

Unity in Duality in humanity as in Nature, which makes the twain one flesh.

These are they of whom Jesus spoke: "For when they shall rise from the dead, they neither marry, nor are they given in marriage; but are as the angels which are in heaven."[7] Naturally such true mates neither marry nor are given in marriage when in the higher realms, for there they are already one, and have been so "from the beginning." It is only while temporarily incarnated on Earth that they have been separated, and therefore need to marry to become one on Earth.

All harmonious and truly happy marriages are those between mates, whether recognized as such or not. And if each Soul truly aspires and asks for its Divine Guidance in this matter it will ultimately but surely be brought into touch with its mate *if that mate is in incarnation*. Most unhappy and mistaken marriages occur either because we do not wait for our guidance to bring our true mate to us, or because we disregard it, or because we mistake old karmic ties—often of brother and sister or mother and son, etc.—for the call of the Soul or because we simply listen to the lusts of the flesh or yield to the call of the world for wealth, position, etc. In such cases we must abide by the conditions we have set up, until we are freed by the laws of the land ere we can seek union with our true mate, or we will have to reap the results of violation of the law, either in this or subsequent lives, thus put-

---

[7] *St. Mark*, XII, 25.

ting off still longer the duty of true spiritual oneness.

But all marriages even between true mates are not necessarily a blissful dream lived without friction; for instead of mates being affinities—that is, alike—they are opposites or complements each of the other, like the right hand and the left, each strong where the other is weak and hence capable not only of seeing each other's deficiencies, but helping to remedy them and being of the greatest help to each other, once they learn to work together. This is often a most difficult lesson to learn unless it is recognized that marriage is a co-partnership in which both must be willing to sacrifice, each for the other, toward the attainment of their common ideal.

Since all persons affect their associates more or less and derive both certain rights and certain obligations from such association, there can be no such thing as absolute freedom where two or more are concerned. Therefore, in entering upon the most intimate, sacred and character-testing of all human relations, both must recognize that they have voluntarily given up their former freedom for the higher state of Unity in Duality. Henceforth neither has the right to act without regard to the other or without considering the effects of their acts upon the other. This does not mean that either should be subordinate to the other, but subordinate to the best good of the two who are now one. Without this willing sacrifice of something of the personality for the good of the duality there can be no true harmonious union of the two.

Today there are many who, awakening to the vital ideal of true marriage, are no longer satisfied with the mere husks or outer conceptions of life so long considered satisfying. They realize that in contracting a marriage the moral and religious aspirations of both the man and the woman should be centered in the same ideals, so that as they evolve and advance toward the realizations of these ideals they may grow ever closer and closer.[8] On the other hand we hear a great deal about "sex equality" and "sex freedom," which have been made the excuse for the unrestrained indulgence of mere animal lust by many so-called "emancipated" women without pretense of love or marriage. This is one result of the extreme swing of the pendulum of "woman's rights."

While there should be "sex equality" in that there should be but one standard of morality for men and women, this slogan should not be made the excuse for woman to adopt the double standard of morality from which she has so bitterly suffered at the hands of man and for which she has justly blamed him. And while the normal monthly cycle of physiological activity of woman's body should naturally give her "sex freedom" to determine when the sacrament of marriage should be consummated, "sex freedom" does not mean that she has the right to indulge her passions with whomsoever she chooses or because she claims to be in "mental harmony" or "numerical oneness" with the object of her desire. For woman's true function is to

---

[8] *The Key to the Universe*, Curtiss, 109.

draw down from its Divine Source, and to conserve and keep to its holiest purposes, the heavenly sap from the Tree of Life. And this can be accomplished only thro true love and perfect purity of mind and body with her own true mate.

When marriage is entered into with this understanding there will be no need to consider such necessarily ineffective palliatives as "trial marriage" or "companionate marriage" in the place of true spiritual marriage; palliatives advocated by those so-called authorities[9] whose every statement shows that they have no conception of the essential spiritual nature of sex and the union of the polar opposites of the twain who are one flesh "from the beginning." The highest conception of such authorities seems to be that marriage means merely the exercise of an animal function or constitutes merely a biological problem or is but a social institution.

There is also a most pernicious doctrine being put forth in certain quarters—more extensively in Europe than in this country, however—and often in the name of "advanced thought" or "esoteric philosophy," that each person is part of a group of seven, with any or all of whom one may have sexual relations without marriage, because the whole group are "soul mates"! It only requires a moment's thought and the most elementary knowledge of morals and philosophy to see the fallacy of such a claim and how it perverts and denies the sublime and spiritual doctrine of Soul Mates

---

[9] *Havelock Ellis, Keyserling, Lindsay,* etc.

as expressed in this volume, and all other truly spiritual teachings. No excuse can be found for this doctrine in either religion or philosophy; for when the sexes were separated the Law of *Duality*—not of *multiplicity*—came into operation and the androgynous Adam was divided into *two* and *not into a group* of seven or any other number. "Male and female created he them. . . . Therefore shall a man leave his father and his mother, and shall cleave unto his wife," that they two may establish a new home which shall be a center of Love and harmony thru which the Divine Creative Force of the Godhead can find expression in humanity.

These tendencies of the so-called "advanced" or radical feminists must be rebuked, discountenanced and rejected by all thinking and right-minded people before they spread beyond the limited few moral radicals who espouse them, or they will lead to the same licentiousness, debauchery and degeneration which caused the fall of Rome, and every other nation which tolerated the violation of the marriage rite and ignored the sacredness of the ideal of the home as the basis of civilization.

These are the days when mankind is reaping that which he has created thru following the doctrines of materialism and the worship of Mammon, making wealth and indulgence of his animal self the supreme attainment of life. Hence many husbands and wives—particularly so-called "modern" women—are asking today, not, Do we love, and if so, how shall we sink unimportant and personal differences in order the better to co-operate lovingly in the one prime essential, the best good of the home? But many are making the division of the family income the sole standard and basis for continuing the marriage and sustaining the home. No wonder, then, that we hear that "marriage is a failure," and some advocate its abolishment or the ignoring of it. But we should realize that these things are but passing phases and extremes which man-kind is reaping as the result of its former misuse and abuse of the marriage relation. Such ideas cannot endure, for mankind cannot get far away from the age-old standards of morals and conduct, advocated by all great religions and found necessary by humanity's experience in all ages, without disaster.

In the marital relations of the present day these spiritual lines of force are woefully mixed and tangled, both thru the Karma of similar mistakes in the past and thru allowing other considerations than Divine Love to bring about a union on the physical plane, thru marriage or otherwise.... But as we enter into the cycle of the new Aquarian Age there must be a great readjustment and untangling process carried out as rapidly as the working out of past relations permits, so that each may return to his or her true spiritual allegiance and make straight the crooked paths of spiritual force, ere the Christ-consciousness can come to each."[10]

When society as a whole has suffered enough from these perversions of the doctrine of the "freedom of

---

[10] *The Key to the Universe*, Curtiss, 111.

the individual" and sets to work in earnest to re-establish the highest standards of mutual love, purity, un-selfishness, forbearance, harmony and co-operation in married life, which is God's plan, it will not take long to brush aside these degenerating fads. In fact the moment mankind recognizes the necessity of returning to the spiritual principles of harmony or Unity in Duality, which underlie the marriage relation as they underlie the universe, and is ready to say that he is tired of eating the husks of life with the swine and is ready to return unto his Father's home where there is enough and to spare, then will he partake of the feast that is prepared for those who love the Lord (Law), "For every true marriage, in which human love reaches up to and blends with Divine Love, is a witness on Earth that Divine Love has been able to penetrate into and manifest thru humanity."[11]

---

[11] *The Key to the Universe*, Curtiss, 106.

CHAPTER XV

SUMMARY

"A stone becomes a plant; a plant a beast; a beast a man; a man a God." *Ancient Kabalistic Axiom.*

"No nation can rise higher than its comprehension of God." *The Message of Aquaria,* Curtiss, 213.

It is obvious to any careful thinker that this planet, our solar system and the galaxy of universes of which our universe is a part did not just happen into existence. And it should be just as obvious to any mind not already biased and prejudiced by preconceived opinions—adopted for the most part because inculcated in youth and not because they have been individually reasoned out—that back of this stupendous manifested universe there must be a Cosmic Purpose, *i.e.*, the perfected expression of the Ideal Type which is the projecting cause back of every manifested form.

That consciousness underlies this great Cosmic Purpose and that a Cosmic Mind expressing Cosmic Consciousness thru a definite, infinitely co-ordinated plan toward a predetermined end, should also be sufficiently obvious once attention has been called to the overwhelming evidence in its favor.

The method of working out the plan for the expression of the Cosmic Purpose is revealed to us in the

SUMMARY

Law of Manifestation which we have tried to outline herein.

The process by which the invisible plan for the perfection of each species is worked out is revealed in the Law of Evolution, *i.e.,* the orderly and progressive—altho not absolutely continuous—advance from the lowest to the highest: from the simple to the complex.

Since the Real Man (Soul) is a spiritual and superphysical being, he does not evolve, but descends more and more perfectly into physical manifestation thru a body which does evolve. This descent or "fall into matter" was a predestined part of the Divine Plan. It was not the result either of a mistake on God's part or of sin on man's part, for it began long before the sexes were separated.

The body thru which the spiritual man must necessarily find expression in matter is the highest example of the animal kingdom, hence does evolve according to the laws of that kingdom.

While man's body is the highest type of animal and the earliest human forms were crude, gigantic and ape-like, man's body did not descend from the ape.

Since man's expression in human form has evolved from the animal kingdom into the human, so must his continued evolution ultimately sweep him from the human into the Super-human kingdom.

Since nothing can manifest on Earth without coming under the Law of Duality, it was inevitable that the incarnating Man or Soul must manifest his masculine and feminine aspects in separated bodies. Sex in man, therefore, inheres in the Soul itself and is not a mere animal function.

Since both masculine and feminine expressions of the Soul are one in essence and have the one Source common to both, it follows that only the one particular man and the one particular woman can be true spiritual mates or manifestations of the one Soul, separate in manifestation but co-operating for perfect expression.

Marriage means the union on Earth of the two who are already one in the higher worlds and have been one "since the beginning of the creation." *True marriage is, therefore, the most important and necessary event in the Souls expression on Earth.*

A true or spiritual marriage can take place only between true mates whose marriage has already been made in heaven, which marriage the human ceremony merely corroborates and sanctions according to the laws of the various countries and communities.

The fact that, by disregarding the inner intuitive voice of the Soul, so many wrong matings have taken place, accounts to a great extent for so many marriages being failures.

The misuse of the creative forces of both mind and body by those who are not mates and the perversion of these forces by wrong thought, lust, etc., is responsible for all the sin, sickness and disease to which the flesh is heir.

Since the flesh is heir to these results of its own creation, it can be free from such results only as humanity recognizes the sanctity of marriage and the sacredness with which the Divine Creative Force manifesting thru man and woman should be used. Only so can they redeem the evil by overwhelming and transmuting it with good.

This is a work of education in which woman, with her superior intuitive powers, should be the leader and inspirer, and upon her devolves the greater responsibility. Until woman thus takes her true place in society she is failing to accomplish her mission on Earth. For as it was woman who led man out of the Garden in Eden, so must it be woman who must teach him how to re-enter it hand in hand with her.

Our study of evolution has shown that it is not a mere mechanical process, but is the physical mechanism by which the invisible Ideal of each type of life finds expression in forms which ever tend toward the expression of perfection.

Finally, as we said in the beginning:[1] If we really understand what evolution means, and if we understand what the *Bible* really says about the origin of man, we will find that there is no conflict between science and religion or between evolution and the *Bible*, only between misconceptions on both sides.

---

[1] See page XI.

SUPPLEMENT

The following chapters were originally issued privately,[1] and while they do not deal directly with evolution or the problems of the Garden in Eden they do deal with the basic concepts of those problems—God and His manifestation within us—hence we feel they may be properly incorporated in this volume.

---

[1] As monthly lessons to the students of the School of Rational Mysticism of *The Order of Christian Mystics*.

CHAPTER XVI

GOD

Part I. The Three-fold Flame— The Father

"It is true that God manifests thru the gradations of His spiritual creatures, for the Creator is omnipresent in His Creation and inseparable from it. Therefore, knowledge of the Creator or true religion, and knowledge of His Creation or exact science, are in their essence one." *Compte de Gabalis*, 96.

"Above the Celestial Fire there is an Incorruptible Flame, ever sparkling, Source of Life, Fountain of all Beings, and Principle of all things. This Flame produces all, and nothing perishes save that which it consumes. This Fire cannot be contained in any place; it is without form and substance. It girdles the Heavens and from it there proceeds a tiny spark which makes the whole fire of the Sun, Moon and Stars. Seek not to know more, for this passes thy comprehension, howsoever wise thou mayest be. Nevertheless, know that the unjust and wicked man cannot hide himself from God, nor can craft nor excuse disguise aught from His piercing eyes. All is full of God. God is everywhere." *Sibylline Oracle*.

In these days of growing disbelief[1] in all things once held sacred, how often do we hear the cry: "You must

---

[1] "An alarming falling off in church membership in Protestant communions at the rate of 500,000 a year is noted in the report of Dr. H. K. Carroll, Secretary of the Continuation Committee of the Interchurch Conference made public today." *Washington Post*, July 30, 1927. A later newspaper account of a report of the federated churches states that among all the Protestant denominations from one quarter to one third of the churches reported not a single new convert for the year 1927!

'show me' before I will believe in any of your religious theories." Science is making such great advances that many are hopelessly divided between believing in the fundamental spiritual truths expounded in the *Bible*, or believing in a wholly materialistic interpretation of the irrefutable facts laid before us by science. Yet, the more science discovers, the less can thinking people accept the orthodox and literal interpretation of the allegories and seeming fables so long revered as Sacred Writ. Therefore, a vital and definite explanation that will include the facts of science is needed.

Among the most fundamental concepts about which there is confusion of mind, and therefore misunderstanding, is the concept of God. We will, therefore, try to give the "show me" people, who are sincerely in earnest in their desire to know, a logical answer which, because correlated with the proved facts of science, should be satisfying to their minds as well as their hearts.

All great scientists agree that back of all manifestation there must be some mighty Intelligence which is the unknown Cause of all, and which governs the universe by definite, purposeful laws which work together toward a predetermined end. It is in the interpretation and explanation of this unknown Cause and Its methods of manifestation that the differences of opinion arise which cause controversy, religion arguing from one standpoint and science from quite another. Since God is infinite and our minds are finite, we can only grasp various aspects of God thru an understanding of some of His manifestations and creations, and from such understanding speculate further as to His essence.

The earliest and most universal concept of God is that which connects Him with light, fire, life and the Sun, and this is the basic concept expounded in the *Bible*, as well as in many of the other great religions and philosophies of the world[2]. "The Lord thy God is a consuming *fire*" (*Deut.*, iv, 24) and, "In him was *life*; and the life was the *light* of men. And the *light* shineth in darkness; and the darkness comprehended it not" (*St. John*, i, 4, 5) are only two of the many such references. Many scientists of the nineteenth century said that all such conceptions belonged to the childhood of the race and must now be abandoned in the light of scientific advance. That, however, was before the discovery of radio-activity and the mysteries of the radiant energy of the atom. Today, as scientists of the Aquarian Age examine the so-called "childish fables" of the past and the so-called "heathen" conceptions of God, they find that the inspired Seers of bygone days in all religions were truly illumined with conceptions of the basic facts of manifestation which the latest scientific researches are only now proving correct, altho those inspired conceptions were often expressed in poetical and allegorical language.

Let us, therefore, begin our inquiry with an effort to find out not Who, but What is God; for God is not a

---

[2] See lesson on "Divine Fire," Curtiss.

person or being, but rather a self-existing, all-pervading Source of radio-active Divine Light, Life, Substance, Consciousness and Love, "whose center is everywhere and whose circumference is nowhere." The physical Sun thru all ages has been recognized as the source of the physical light, warmth and magnetic life-force of our planet, and thus has naturally and universally been connected with the idea of God as fire. The Sun, Moon and stars were considered as but manifested sparks of the one Divine or Celestial Fire of the Cosmos, whose Source was the invisible Spiritual Sun called "the Sun behind the Sun." St. Paul tells us, "There is one glory of the sun, and another glory of the moon, and another glory of the stars; for one star differeth from another star in glory,"[3] showing that all are but various manifestations of the one Divine Radiance, God.

The presence of fire or warmth in some degree is absolutely essential to every manifestation of life, for without it all is cold, lifeless and dead. And at absolute zero (-273° C.) scientists tell us all manifestation ceases, the atoms then being entirely at rest. Therefore, life itself is rightly regarded as a form or manifestation of fire. And since fire is an aspect of Divine Radiance, all life is a manifestation of God, so that wherever there is life there is God in manifestation. "If I ascend up into heaven thou art there: if I make my bed in hell, behold, thou art there. If I take the wings of the morning, and dwell in the

---

[3] *I Corinthians*, XV, 41.

uttermost parts of the sea; even there shall thy hand lead me, and thy right hand shall hold me."[4]

This doctrine should not be confused with pantheism, for while God is immanent in all His creations, since no one creation, nor all of them combined, can express all of God, He is also transcendent.

The Sibylline Oracles tell us that: "There is in God an immense depth of Flame. The heart must not, however, fear to touch this adorable Fire nor to be touched by it. It will be in no wise consumed by this gentle Flame, whose peaceful warmth causes the union, harmony and duration of the world. Nothing exists save by this Fire, which is God himself. . . . This is God; as for us we are His Messengers. We are but a little part of God."[5] This may be called a 'heathen' idea of God, yet it is a more illuminating and comprehensive description of God than the ordinary mind can gather from many of the Hebrew expressions about God found in the *Bible*. There is a very narrow, provincial and conceited idea abroad in much of Christendom that all who are not Christians, and all the countless millions who lived before the Christian era, are and were 'heathen' and therefore not in touch with or under the care of God. As if God had never revealed Himself or taught, guided and comforted humanity before the Christian era! Yet the researches of comparative religion show that there never was a time when humanity was not watched over, guided

---

[4] *Psalms*, CXXXIX, 8, 9.
[5] *Compte de Gabalis*, 70.

and inspired of God. The only 'heathen' are those who neglect or refuse to worship their highest conception of God. And we do not have to go to foreign countries to find them!

"The Philosophers hold that the relation of the Creator has been the same in all ages; that all creeds evolved by man *are but man's concept* of this relation and in no wise alter it; that the Truth regarding the Fatherhood of God, Sonship of His Messengers, the great Teachers of humanity, and Brotherhood of all His creatures, is superior to creeds and religions, and will unify them when once apprehended."[5]

From a study of the flame we may arrive at a better understanding of the three-fold nature of God or the Trinity, the one God manifesting in three aspects, but not persons. Every flame has three aspects: (a) the invisible essence or spirit of the flame, (b) the light of the flame, and (c) its heat or warmth. We are told that God is Spirit and that we must worship Him in Spirit and in Truth. This is the "cold flame" of Divine Radiance which is the unseen Fire of all life, and is known only by its effects as it gives life to all things, to each according to the degree of its individual development. This is the Father aspect of God and finds its correspondence in the inner, invisible essence of the flame, from which both its heat and light proceed.

Surrounding this inner, invisible core is the bright,

vivid light of the flame, which gives it its individuality. This corresponds to the individualized manifestations of God thru His Son, the Christos, who is very appropriately called the Light of the World; that manifestation which can be seen of men in the physical world as the Sun in the heavens, which gives light and life to all physical forms and purifies and redeems those that are disintegrating. In the spiritual world He is seen as the Christ, the Avatar, both the Light of the World and the Redeemer of Mankind, who is periodically manifested in human form to give spiritual light and life to all mankind. This projection of the Divine to manifest phenomenally as the Son of God in human form among men is possible approximately every 2,000 years when the physical Sun comes into conjunction with the Spiritual Sun, at which time the influence of the Spiritual Sun or "the Sun behind the Sun" is most potent upon the Earth. "Then, gathering to itself the power of its own Source and transmitting it through our Sun to this Planet, it is said to send the Sons of God into the consciousness of the earth sphere that a new world of thought and emotion may be born in the minds of men for the stimulation of humanity's spiritual evolution. Such a manifestation marks the beginning or end of an epoch upon Earth by the radiation of that divine consciousness known as the Christ Ray or Paraclete."[6]

The heat of the flame, which alone makes any manifestation of life possible, corresponds to the warmth

---

[6] *Compte de Gabalis*, 88.

of Divine Love, that Immortal Love of the Divine Mother, the Bringer Forth of all those manifestations which were impregnated in the various forms of life by the Father. This is the Holy Ghost or the Comforter of whom Jesus said: "It is expedient that I go away; for if I go not away, the Comforter will not come unto you."[7] Thus the three-fold flame is an example and illustration of the Trinity; a three-fold manifestation of the one Divine Radiance which man calls God.

Quite naturally man's worship of God has followed three main types, the three Persons of the Trinity. In the earliest days after his introduction to this newly made planet, man naturally worshipped God the Father, the fiery Flame whose mighty power he felt and the terrific force of whose outbreathing he saw. It was dimly realized that there was a law back of all manifestation, the authority of the Father, which must be obeyed, often in fear and trembling. This naturally led to the authority of the human father as the head of the family, whose word was law.

After long ages this form of worship gave way to the worship of the Divine Mother, as exemplified especially in Egypt under the name of Isis, in India under the name of Devaki and in the Christian religion as Mary. In their aspect as the Bringer Forth, both Nature and the Earth were worshipped as a Mother whose products feed and nourish the children of her bosom as a mother's milk does her babe. Among

---

[7] *St. John*, XVI, 7.

the enlightened this was not a materialistic worship of Nature itself, but of the Divine Mother as expressed thru Nature. During the ages when the worship of the Divine Mother reigned, mankind was guided largely by inspired priestesses or Sibyls whose oracles were considered, and often truly were, expressions of the guidance of the Divine Mother, as the records of the Oracles clearly show. For divine inspiration has ever been and ever will continue to be God's chief avenue of expression for the guidance of humanity. But it can be given only thru those sincere and devoted Souls whose lives and whose unfolded higher faculties are truly attuned to varying degrees of God-consciousness, and enable them to reach up into the higher realms of God-consciousness and bring down to humanity higher conceptions of eternal principles for its guidance.

The worship of the Father and the Mother is slowly superseded by the worship of the Son, which gradually takes precedence over all other forms; in the Western world as the worship of Jesus, in Egypt of Horus, in India of Krishna, Buddha, etc., all of whom are called "the Light of the World and the Redeemer of Mankind." The worship of these three aspects of the Trinity greatly overlaps each other and hence may be found simultaneously, not only in humanity in general, but in the same nation and even in the same religion. The change from the worship of one aspect to that of another is thus prophesied by the Oracle at Delphi shortly before it ceased. "Alas, Tripods! Weep and make funeral oration for your Apollo. He is mortal. He expires; because the Light of the Celestial Flame (the Christos) extinguishes him." And, "Eusebius cites Porphyry as saying that since Jesus began to be worshipped no man has received any public help or benefit from the gods";[8] that is, thru the Sibyls, as formerly. This is only natural, for, with the manifestation of the Christos, the Son of the Father-Mother—the Light of the Flame of the Spiritual Sun—a new era had dawned when humanity had to recognize and learn to worship the same one God in the person of His Son.

The whole universe is, therefore, the product of three mighty streams of force that are passing thru all things like a life-line that is sent out into all the realms and all the worlds and all the systems, bringing with it life and love and understanding. The Father is the great reservoir of life from which all things emanate and yet which is absolutely void of productiveness and creation unless joined to the Mother. The Mother is the great mighty stream of Love, immortal Divine Love; that Love which goes out and out and out and carries with it the life-stream which some call the great magnetic stream, vivifying it, electrifying it, making it productive. From this stream there comes forth that which we call the Son-force, the result, the product or the thing that is brought forth by the Father-Mother. This life and love, this Father-Mother, never ask us to help Them bring forth.

---

[8] *Compte de Gabalis*, 96.

They bring forth in us just as They bring forth in Nature.

We should think of these two forces uniting in us and realize that then within us is born the Son of God. We do not have to struggle and pray and ask, in fact our struggling but delays its manifestation. Our mental anguish, our arguing with ourselves, our self-analysis, our complaints, all are but boulders in the stream, damming it up and holding it back. Let it flow. Get the attitude of mind that the Father-Mother knows what we need. We need the birth within us of this immortal Son, the Son of God in humanity. Try to think of ourselves as children of this Father-Mother force. Try to realize that it is this force that has brought forth the universe, that it is this force that is ever perfecting all creation; the mighty Love of the Mother, the everlasting power of the Father. Let us say to ourselves: "This universal everlasting power is in me, it fills me; fills every atom of my body. There is no particle of sand or earth or deep place in the universe where this stream of life and love does not penetrate. Therefore, there is no spot in my body, my brain, my hands, my heart, that is not penetrated and filled with this force. Life and Love fill me. Then why should I be afraid? If Life and Love are universal they could not be universal unless they were within me. That would be imperfection."

Do we ever stop to think that That which we call God, the universal Father-Mother, would be imperfect without us? If we refuse to let Them fill us; if we let our little personal ideas, our little worries, our little arrangements of things in our own minds, if we let all this dam up the stream, we are depriving the great loving Mother and the ever-living Father of that which is Their own. Therefore, since we are filled with this force and since this force is and must be universal, eternal and omnipotent, then let us take away the barriers and open the little door in our hearts. This understanding can never come thru the head or the brain. It must be something in our hearts that opens and responds.

We are told that "God is a consuming fire," yet also that "God is Love," and we are apt to think of the God of Love as the ruler of heaven and God the consuming fire as the ruler of hell, until in the minds of many there seem to be two Gods, one a Supreme Being and the other His opponent, the devil, to whom more worship, in the way of propitiation, is given than to God. The explanation of this paradox is simple if we remember that God as Love is the feminine, constructive, nourishing and integrating aspect of God, while God as a consuming Fire is that aspect which is bringing redemption out of disintegration.

Cosmically the forces of the planets manifest cyclically in a three-fold manner. For instance, the cycle of this planet began with the projection of a Ray (the Father aspect) of the Divine Flame which was so universally worshipped by the ancients. Not only was this Earth awakened into activity by this Ray of Divine Fire, but that invisible Ray guided and moulded the seething mass of fire-mist from which the physical planet was condensed,[9] and prepared it for the other aspects of the Flame—the various forms and manifestations of the Life—which were later to be brought forth upon it. These various stages of preparation consumed vast eons of what man calls time, yet they are clearly summarized in a few cryptic verses in *Genesis*.

The cleansing process of the Divine Flame in each Age has first to prepare the Earth and all humanity for the New Day during the dark night which precedes the coming dawn. For only when conditions for its unobstructed manifestation are prepared can the adorable beauty of the Light of the World begin to manifest and be perceived of mankind.

How many of us are now ready for the recognition of the new Manifestation so soon to come? And, if we are not, how can we prepare ourselves for it? Among other things we can repeat the *Prayer for Light*[10] each day upon awakening and meditate upon it until we fill ourselves with that Light, that it shall radiate from us throughout the day. At noon we may repeat the *Prayer to the Divine Mother*. And in the evening, as we see the Sun just touching the horizon in the west, we can repeat the *Evening Prayer* and try to carry the consciousness of it with us into the higher realms during sleep. As we thus repeatedly and per-

---

[9] See chapter on "World Chains," *The Voice of Isis*, Curtiss, 204.
[10] See Appendix to *Letters from the Teacher*, or *The Message of Aquaria*, Curtiss.

sistently correlate our consciousness with the three aspects or persons of the Godhead, or the three aspects of the Divine Flame, we will gradually prepare ourselves to become Knights of the Holy Grail, that we may understandingly and wisely help to radiate or shed abroad the mystic Blood (the Divine Life-force) of the Christ, for the redemption of mankind and the Earth.

PRAYER FOR LIGHT

O Christ! Light Thou within my heart
The Flame of Divine Love and Wisdom,
That I may dwell forever
In the Radiance of Thy countenance
And rest in the Light of Thy smile.

PRAYER TO THE DIVINE MOTHER

Divine Mother!
Illumine me with Divine Wisdom,
Vivify me with Divine Life and
Purify me with Divine Love,
That in all I think and say and do
I may be more and more Thy child.

EVENING PRAYER

As the physical Sun disappears from our sight
May the Spiritual Sun arise in our hearts,
Illumine our minds
And shed its radiant blessing
Upon all we contact.

CHAPTER XVII

GOD

Part II. The Chariot of Fire — The Divine Mother

"Behold, there appeared a chariot of fire and horses of fire. . . . and Elijah went up by a whirlwind into heaven."
II Kings, II, 11.

"Swing low, sweet chariot, comin' for to carry me home.
Swing low, sweet chariot, comin' for to carry me home.
I looked over Jordan and what did I see?
Comin' for to carry me home?
A band of angels comin' after me, comin' for to carry me home." *Negro Spiritual*.

All manifestation takes place according to definite cosmic laws. And since physical life is but an outer manifestation of an inner, invisible life-force which emanates from the cosmic Source of the universal One Life, and we see the entire cosmos manifest as though breathed out by the Breath of God, it is easy to realize that each phase of manifestation or life-cycle represents a new cyclic outbreathing or cyclic renewal of God-expression. Therefore, we do not have to delve into abstruse scientific evidence to conclude that all Nature is but one of the manifold expressions of God.

The Manifestation of the Spiritual Sun or "Sun behind the Sun" is called the Chariot of the Sun, the Chariot of Fire or the Fire of the Lord. This Chariot of Fire periodically descends low to Earth approximately every 2,000 years. As the first effect of the Sun in Spring is to melt the banks of snow, thaw out the ground and purify the Earth of the débris accumulated during the Winter, so the first effect of the Chariot of Fire is to melt the rigid, set and crystallized habits, customs, ideas and conditions among mankind: to melt the heart and purify the minds of humanity and bring a new outpouring of the three-fold aspect of God—Divine Light, Life and Love—which shall enable the soil of men's hearts to bring forth anew the seeds of their higher possibilities and powers, to renew their spiritual life for a new season of growth and expression. This also carries home to the heart of the Godhead the fruits of the last Age (Piscean) thru which the world has just passed.

As this Chariot of Fire draws close to Earth of, necessity mighty changes must take place; changes[1] in the Earth itself, comparable to the breaking up of winter and the thawing of the ground; changes in the thought, life, customs and institutions of humanity, comparable to revolution in all phases of life: in science, industry, economics, in society, government and religion. The chaff of former seasons, the husks or outer forms which once held grains of truth, must now be cast aside as the new grain begins to sprout for the New Age. All outgrown forms or expressions of truth

---

[1] See *Coming World Changes*, Curtiss.

—whether scientific, philosophical or religious—must be gathered up and consumed by the new outbreathing of the Fire of the Lord, just as the farmer gathers up and burns the weeds and trash of the past season that all the good which remains—the mineral salts of the ashes—may go to enrich the soil for the coming season. Just so must the weeds humanity has allowed to grow and the trash which civilization has allowed to accumulate be consumed, that whatsoever of good it contains may go to enrich the soil of mankind and help the spiritual seeds of love, compassion, co-operation and helpful service to spring forth, that the seeds of good lying dormant in the hearts of even the most unevolved and the seemingly debased may awaken into life as man's life and understanding are enriched by mistakes corrected, faults overcome and trials and tests bravely borne.

This Chariot of Fire represents the same Power that enveloped Elijah and carried him up to heaven out of the sight of Elisha and the fifty sons of the prophets of Jericho. It is the same Cloud by day and Pillar of Fire by night that led the Children of Israel thru the wilderness; the same Cloud of Glory that took Jesus up out of the sight of His disciples at His ascension. As in the case of Elisha, only hearts attuned to the mightiness of this Divine Flame can see or understand the radiance of one who has entered the Chariot of Fire. For this Chariot is none other than the descent of the Shekinah, "by which we understand the presence of the Holy Spirit, speaking and communicating itself to men by revelation."[2] Its descent assures us of the possibility of our so correlating with the higher aspects of our Soul qualities that we can be lifted up and illumined as in a Chariot of Fire.

To the Initiates into the Mysteries of all religions this Chariot of Fire is well known, for there are certain ceremonies of the Mysteries which cannot be performed until the priests, by chanting certain especially arranged *mantras* and lifting up and attuning their consciousness to the key-note of the higher realms, are able to see the Chariot of Fire descend as a Cloud of Glory over the sanctuary and give them the powers necessary for the ceremony.

Today as the cosmic Chariot again draws near that the Son of God, the Light of the World, the Christos, may step forth among mankind, its fiery steeds start down the steep descent which marks the close of a cosmic day or Age (the Piscean), and a dark night-period must be passed ere the Earth can awaken to the New Day in a new chamber of the zodiac (Aquarius). The decree has been sent forth from on high: "Gather the grain into the garner, but burn the chaff with unquenchable fire." The unquenchable fire is the Fire of the Lord in its consuming aspect, which must consume the husks of civilization's past age: everything that prevents man's spiritual evolution and a higher and truer expression of God's Divine Plan. The great lesson that man must learn, slowly at first but in all its fullness as the New Age advances,

---

[2] *Calmet's Bible Dictionary*, 821.

is the true meaning of the Fatherhood of God, the Brotherhood of Man thru the presence of His Son, and the all-pervading, ever-enduring Love and power of the Divine Mother to bring forth good out of evil.

We speak of the warmth of Love, thus recognizing it as a manifestation of Divine Fire; the everlasting Fire that makes the Earth a living thing, bringing forth in beauty and abundance when the fire of the Sun is tempered by water; that Fire which will not consume, but illumine, unfold and manifest the God-like qualities of whosoever correlates with it. For this reason insincere or simulated love, and its corollaries, false sympathy and compassion, are easily detected by one who is at all sensitive, for when not genuine they have no Soul warmth or sparks of Divine Fire in them.

But love can be the most devastating force in the world in our character, in our lives and in humanity if we turn it outside in and vilify it; if we call love something vile; if we identify it with the passions of the animal body and seek to stifle instead of purifying and uplifting them; if we seek to push it aside and say: "The mind is all-important. The ancient teachings are all-important." What has brought the world into the state in which we find it today? Largely these same ancient teachings that will have nothing to do with new ideas, new conceptions and new realizations of God; these, together with the medieval conceptions of the teachings of Christ; false interpretations of the message of the God of Love, which identify love with passion and seek to kill it out. Hence we must be open to new interpretations that are in harmony with the advances of the age in which we live, if we would progress wisely.

If we seek to confine this Divine Fire to its lowest avenues of expression, such as love of self, love of possessions, love of sexual indulgence, etc., it becomes a devastating and consuming fire; for it so transcends those limited avenues that it burns them out when confined to them.

Just so with the Earth. When water (the Love of the Divine Mother) does not commingle with the fiery force of the Sun (Father) the Earth is burned and becomes a barren desert. Yet even in its burning aspect it is still Divine Fire operating thru the Law as Karma to bring to humanity a realization of the vital truth which it must ultimately learn, *i.e.,* that the tares which it has allowed to grow among the wheat must be consumed, that from their ashes the misdirected life-force may be redeemed for the good of all.

Therefore, while in one aspect God is a consuming Fire, we must never forget that He is also Divine Love; a Love so mighty, so long-suffering and so capable of seeing the true inwardness of man's intent, and the reason for his failures, that in Divine Compassion man is repeatedly given new opportunities to respond to that Love. Humanity as a whole is also periodically given such opportunities. This new Aquarian Age is just such a new opportunity for man to face his True Self and once more choose whether he will ally himself with and be guided by the Love of the inner Divine Self or be led astray by the lower temporal loves of the temporary and evanescent human personality. Hence those of the new Aquarian Age, like those at the beginnings of all former Ages, must face the living Flame of God-the-Father in all its fiery, cleansing, transmuting and regenerating aspects.

By learning this great lesson that "God is Love"—love in all its aspects—we can understand how the "Fire of the Lord" can consume, transmute and evolve the base metals of human frailties into the pure gold of spiritual attainment. When the warmth of this Flame of Divine Love is recognized by a mortal it arouses a glow of adoration and awe. For the mortal consciousness has, to that extent, united itself to a vibration of the Divine. And this response, even though at first temporary, brings added life, new understanding, illumined inspiration and protection to all who recognize and give expression to it. This is one explanation of the mantra: "Thy banner over me is love."

While cosmically the Chariot of Fire descends for the purification, illumination and regeneration of mankind as a whole, only every 2,000 years, as it is doing today, yet the rays of its power descend individually to every heart that attunes itself to the Divine Flame, no matter how intellectually ignorant or sorrowful or hopeless that one may be. In fact, it is more often such so-called simple Souls who are apt to call down the Fire of the Lord and recognize the touch of the

Divine Flame than those who have attained great intellectual development and high position in the world at the expense of their heart qualities. For to enter the Chariot of Fire we do not need to scale mountains of learning or delve deep into the relics of ancient lore thru ponderous tomes of other men's thoughts, thru expressions of wisdom suitable for bygone ages but not for today, nor seek wisdom among the dead and outgrown conceptions of ancient schools of thought, seeking the ever-living Flame among the ashes of the past. We can enter the Chariot by lighting the Flame within our own hearts here and now.

There is a well-known yet very primitive song, the refrain of which is quoted at the head of this lesson, "Swing low, sweet chariot, comin' for to carry me home." This song deeply touches the hearts of most persons. Its simple faith, its primitive pathos and plaintive melody awaken in them a vibration or vague memory of something only too apt to be pushed aside as childish or mere imagination. It touches the emotions because it awakens a Soul-cry from the depths of the human heart; the cry of a Soul lost in the desert of the outer material life; the cry to be carried back to Its real home, Its spiritual home.

This Chariot that we ask to swing low is the mighty on-rushing power of the Shekinah, the invisible manifestation of the three-fold Godhead; a living power that descends from the Throne of God, into whose current of fiery force we seek to step, there to rest in its wondrous power, be comforted by its tender love and be renewed by its mighty strength, be our path or condition in the outer life what it may.

When things of the outer life no longer satisfy and former friends fail us, if we cry out from our hearts, "Swing low, sweet Chariot," the mighty God-love sends down a Ray of this Chariot into our hearts to lift us up to the heart of the Divine Mother, the Comforter, whose tender Love can wipe away all tears, all sorrow, all trace of sin from our consciousness, leaving the Great Law as Karma to work out the outer adjustment. For what is Karma but the working out of mistakes by giving the Soul a new opportunity, thru drawing a new breath of Life, to face and solve the same problems it failed to solve or to conquer the temptations to which it yielded before, with the new strength and understanding gained by a sojourn in the home of Love, between incarnations?

Once we learn, as all ultimately must, that the Fire of the Lord is but the outshining of that Divine Radiance destined to consume all evil, purify the good and transmute the dross into pure gold, we have learned one of our chief lessons in life. How eagerly then will we cry out, "Swing low, sweet Chariot"! For we realize that it is the living Cloud of Glory which surrounds the altar of the Most High; which lifts up the hearts of all desolate ones out of mortal sight; which can lift us, the Real Inner Self, out of the physical body for the time being, out of all sordid physical conditions and carry us home, home, where we can kneel in the great Temple of the Sun of Suns while the living Flame licks around our empty bodies and purifies, refines and glorifies them.

Then the Chariot becomes not a consuming fire from which we shrink back appalled, but the mighty Flame of God-love burning in the hearts of all who can recognize it as the warming, life-giving Fire of Love. It comes to us on the wings of the great Bird of Life at our call; for it is real Life to all who lay down the burdens of self and the attractions of the world and cry out to be taken to their real home where they can see God face to face, not after death, but here and now. Then the Chariot of Fire fills us with enthusiasm instead of fear; with burning zeal to do the will of the Father; with eager desire to help on the work of the illumination and regeneration of humanity; a willingness that the Flame shall burn from us all personal faults and failings, whether it carries us into the thickest of the fray or into the desolate deserts of life.

Once we have entered into this Chariot all our faculties and God-powers are stimulated and begin to unfold. No longer is our intellect coldly analytical and critical, but flaming with love which makes our words of cheer and comfort burn into the hearts of our hearers. It fills us with life and strength and vigor. Henceforth life is real and earnest, for the Chariot of Fire has carried us home, to our true spiritual home, to the heart of the Divine. The spiritual home of each Soul is not the old-fashioned idea of a psalm-singing, innocuous bliss where we loaf our time away in idleness, but is that higher spiritual consciousness in which we realize the reason for our existence; realize our real place in life and our true work to accomplish in the world, both within ourselves and within our environment, no matter in what outer circumstances we may find ourselves and no matter what outer trials and difficult experiences we may have to pass through. When we understand this how gladly will we cry, "Swing low, sweet Chariot, so low that I may step in, that Thy mighty power may carry me home to the heart of God where I can see my place and my part in the Divine Plan and gain the power of the Flame to accomplish it."

Thus must the Chariot of Fire ever swing low at the call of the Soul, so close to Earth that it can carry home those children of Earth who are ready. For only those who have been carried home and been filled with Divine Love can in their turn pour out that Love for the help of mankind; to touch their hearts, bring hope to the discouraged and comfort and cheer to the sorrowing. For this world—God's world which He loves with a mighty yearning to save—can never be saved by cold intellectuality, by sarcasm or pomposity or by great claims or the suggestion of "I am holier than thou. I am the Chosen One, hence know it all." God does not say to His children, "Kneel down before me and worship at my feet." God does not say, "Gaze upon me and be abased, for I am mighty and you are insignificant." Rather does God say, "You are my loved children, made in my image and after my likeness." And what is this image[3] and likeness? It certainly is not the outer body of flesh and blood, but is the inner three-fold Flame of Divinity hidden within the secret chamber of our hearts; the Power of the Father, the Love of the Mother and the Light of the Christos combined into a three-fold Flame. It may be but like a babe in a cradle, covered up for a time perhaps, unknown and unsuspected, yet vitally alive and capable of being uncovered and developed; capable of awakening in us Divine Realization and proving to us that we are Divine; capable of taking control of our minds and guiding our lives if only recognized and obeyed.

---

[3] See *Chapter XIX*, herein.

CHAPTER XVIII

GOD

Part III. The Christos — The Son

"For God so loved the world, that he gave his only begotten Son, that whosoever believeth in him should not perish, but have everlasting life." *St. John*, III, 16.

"All things are delivered onto me of my Father: and no man knoweth the Son but the Father; neither knoweth any man the Father, save the Son, *and he to whomsoever the Son will reveal Him.*" *St. Matthew*, XI, 27.

In our first lesson on God we considered Him as a three-fold Flame, the three persons of the Trinity. We also considered Him as the Father, the Creative Power which projected all things into manifestation: that Power which becomes the transmuting and consuming Fire of the Lord for all forms when their cycle of manifestation has ended. In the second lesson we considered God as the Divine Mother, the Chariot of Fire, which in infinite love and tenderness is sent down into sinning and sorrowing humanity—as the Comforter who welcomes to Her bosom all who will look up and recognize Her and step into Her Chariot, and who will carry them back to their real home, the loving Heart of Divinity. There they will be comforted, refreshed and taught of God. There they will hear

Him say, "Neither do I condemn thee: go, and sin no more."

In this lesson we will consider God in His third aspect, the Christos, the only begotten Son who is sent forth to manifest in human form because of the crying need of His ignorant children for a new realization of the meaning of Emmanuel or "God with us," a manifestation of God which they can see and touch and hear with their physical senses.

While we consider God thus under three aspects for explanatory purposes we must remember that these three are one, just as we may consider a man as a kind father watching over, protecting and providing for his children; and the same man in loving, tender oneness with his wife, the mother of his children, the home-maker and comforter, whose loving sympathy helps him to forget the cares and worries of the day and whose love, like a Chariot of Fire, carries him into the peace and comfort of the home where his heart is; and the same man as a dutiful and obedient son gladly following in the footsteps of a wise and loving father whom he reveres. These three markedly different aspects are not three different men, only three different aspects of the same man manifested to meet different needs and conditions. Just so are the three persons of the Trinity three aspects of the one God.

It is very significant that the word begotten is used in the Nicene Creed when referring to the Son: "Begotten of the Father. . . . begotten, not made, of one substance with the Father, by whom all things were made." This gives the correct, transcendental and cosmic view of the Son as a Divine Being; not a mere mortal who became illumined, but the universal Principle of Divine Light and Life, the Christos.[1] "In him was life; and the life was the light of men." This spiritual Son bears to humanity somewhat the same relation that the physical Sun bears to the planet; for just as the Sun is the source of all physical light and heat for the whole planet, so does the spiritual Son fill with warmth and spiritual light everyone who is born into the world, whether they recognize and respond to that light or not.

This is the Christ-seed which is planted in the soil of every heart. Altho it may lie dormant, unrecognized and unmanifested for a long time, some day in some incarnation there is bound to come a spiritual Springtime when this Christ-seed will begin to put out shoots and grow and manifest in the life and consciousness.

Hence, no one can say he or she is left out because so humble and insignificant, any more than the humblest weed in the garden is left out of the sunshine because it is not a cultivated flower. All creation was intended to work in harmony with and minister to the evolution of its crowning achievement, man, that he might awaken to the Light of the Christos within him "and have dominion over.... every living thing that moveth upon the earth."

---

[1] For a fuller explanation see Chapter XIV, "Jesus and the Christ," in *Letters from the Teacher*, Curtiss, Vol. II.

Note how the Power of the Father has provided for every need of His children: every wholesome thing to furnish us food, and healing essences of herb and mineral provided ages in advance for all possible future ills. Note how the Love of the Divine Mother provides the beauties of flower and tree and sky and sea to thrill us with joy and happiness: how She comforts us with Her tender Love as a mother nestles her babe over her heart. Every mother who bears a child carries it in a Chariot of Fire close to her heart until it is ready to enter the sphere of its life in the outer world, there to partake of the blessings so bountifully provided. Just so does the Divine Mother carry us in Her Chariot of Fire—the Divine Womb—until we are born spiritually and are willing and eager to take up the work given us by the Father. Note how the Light of the Son illumines our mind, expands our consciousness and enlarges our capacity both to comprehend that Light and to use all things in the outer life to manifest His glory.

Go out in the early morning, after a long drought has been broken by a copious rain during the night, and see how the earth rejoices in its refreshing. See how the Sun shines forth as a benison of love, and thrill at the miracle that has bloomed forth from what but yesterday was a desolate waste of dry and withered foliage. Then realize that the uprushing of the same life-force of the Christos which has wrought such a miracle, when merely diffused throughout Nature, can perform a still greater miracle when focused in us.

For we are so far advanced beyond all other forms in Nature that the Christ light and life is individualized in us and can therefore unfold in and through us the pattern of the inner Self, the Divine Man.

Realize that to the degree that we respond to the urge of the Christ within will It illumine our entire being, opening the tiny buds of the Christ-consciousness in us—so often lying concealed and dormant in the sacred centers of our bodies—just as the Sun opens the hidden sprouts of the rose until they push out from a seemingly dead branch, first as buds so tiny, then, as they drink in the rain and absorb the Sun, gradually unfold and begin to show their color until the rose finally becomes a thing of beauty, and the essence of its heart perfumes the air to the joy of all. This is a marvelous lesson for man to learn; for, just as the physical life-force unfolds the centers of the rose to the perfection of its inner pattern, so can the spiritual life-force of the Son of God unfold in us the Image of God, with all the gifts, faculties and powers which the Father has built into man's divine pattern.

All these God-powers are built into our bodies as seeds of Christhood, hidden in the seven sacred centers, but they remain undeveloped until the outer man begins to recognize and correlate with the Christ within. Then these germs of divinity begin to sprout and put forth, and ultimately unfold the Image of God within until we are able to demonstrate that we are Sons of God. "The spirit itself beareth witness with our spirit, that we are children of God; and if children, then heirs: heirs of God, and joint heirs with Christ."[2] This is the only way safely to unfold these sacred centers; to grow as the flower grows. To open them forcibly or prematurely thru special exercises, is like tearing open the bud of the rose.

In the allegorical language of the *Bible* these sacred centers in the body constitute the manger or those centers of life-force to which the animal nature comes for its food, but in the midst of which the Christ is laid at the moment of His birth, or when the realization of the Christ takes place within our consciousness. This unfoldment is the fruit of the Tree of Life—spinal cord—planted in the midst of our Garden, thru which, if we "feed on it in our hearts with prayer and thanksgiving," we shall attain eternal life.

To unfold these centers of Christ-force we do not have to turn our backs upon the beauties of Nature or forego all the happiness and joys of life with which God has surrounded us, and the faculties for whose enjoyment God has built into our mind and body. Much less do we have to despise the wonderful body God has given us or starve and abuse the flesh and crucify ourselves with false conceptions of God's Love and His desires for us which were thought necessary during the Dark Ages, any more than we have to follow the opinions of the Dark Ages now in other fields of life. Nor do we have to go thru the years of self-immolation, cruel torture and degradation which many ancient

---

[2] *Romans*, VIII, 16-17.

teachings hold is the only true preparation for Christhood.

For the true mystic there is no elaborate ceremonial needed, no wearisome series of exercises and difficult mental concentration necessary; only a constant permitting of his love to flow to the Christ because he cannot help it: only a lifting up of the Christ out of the manger where He is now hidden and where the food for the animal man is now doubly blessed because He has manifested in the midst of it. Then we must unwrap the swaddling clothes and hold Him aloft and cry aloud: "Oh, Lord Christ, Thou art the source of my life, my light, my wisdom and my joy. Thou art the power which shall unfold my consciousness to realize Thy presence so I can manifest Thy glory to the world. Unto Thee I dedicate my atoms, my body, my mind, my service, my life forevermore. Amen." The realization of the Christ within is the work for each individual heart, but the embodiment of the Christos in human form is a work for humanity as a whole.

If we strive to unfold our mystic centers for their own sake, for the sake of gaining super-normal powers; if we force their development thru concentration, breathing exercises, negative "sitting for development" with the aid of discarnate astral beings, the centers thus unfolded will admit us only into the astral or psychic world. But when we seek their unfoldment as channels for service to and the manifestation of the Christ within then they admit us into the Christ-consciousness and the spiritual world.

Just as the Sun, when shining upon fertile soil well supplied with water—the love-force in Nature—will bring forth perfect fruit, so will the Son, the Spiritual Sun, shining in our hearts—if we open our consciousness to its radiance and water them with the tenderness of love—bring forth the perfect fruit of the Christ-seed implanted within all. For he who realizes God in his heart, God in his mind, God in his body, has health and strength and understanding and illumination and contentment. These are those who find that they do not have to separate themselves from life to find the Christ; who do not need learned teachers, nor abstruse treatises, nor mysterious, hidden teachings handed down from long-past ages when the study of higher truths was punishable by torture and hence they were taught only thru mysterious symbols and allegories: teachings which held that mankind was too wicked to live among, hence those who were ready for higher truths must withdraw into retreats, must sacrifice all that was beautiful and joyous in life and become abnormal. That is not the path of the mystic.

As we enter this new Aquarian Age all that is necessary is to come, first into an understanding and then into a realization of the Son of God, the beloved Christ which has been within us and seeking for recognition from the beginning. All we need to do is to realize, morning, noon and night, that God is Love, God is Light, God is Life, and that this three-fold God is within us, even though as yet unborn to our conscious realization. Let us say to ourselves: "I will take this babe, now wrapped in the hampering swaddling clothes of misconception and misunderstanding, now called by names that are not His own, who is looked upon by humanity as something to be hidden and ashamed of or only half expressed, and I will lift Him up in my consciousness and support and protect Him with the strength of a father who would that his child become a useful and important citizen. I will cherish Him with the tenderness of a mother who suckles her babe at her breast."

Is this difficult to do? It does not require a sage or a yogi to understand it. It is so simple that man-kind has almost lost sight of it under the clouds of theology that have gathered around it. For the learned ones have cried: "Give me something mystical, something great! Tell me how to climb the heights, not how to seek in a manger! Tell me how to trample upon or drive out the animals from the stable (the natural functions of the body). Tell me how to mortify the flesh that I may attain spirituality!" They have striven to repress all joy in life and have striven to become beggars and hermits. They have said to themselves, "Here am I in the midst of a wicked world." And then they have helped to make it more wicked by separating the gift from the Giver; by throwing back into His face the Love given them as a part of Himself; by refusing to enjoy the beautiful world with which He has surrounded them and the wonderful body He has provided for their use. As well might we strip the buds from a rose and expect it to bloom.

Let us stop and think who gave us this body, with all its organs and functions. God Himself. And surely He did not give it to us to be despised and abused, but to be used as a vehicle, a physical instrument that is absolutely necessary if the Christ within is to manifest thru us in Earth conditions. For this body of ours contains centers thru which we can contact and ultimately express all the God-faculties and God-powers which we—the Real or Spiritual Self—inherit as sons and daughters of God, created in His image and after His likeness. If it were not that we must ultimately manifest these higher faculties and powers there would have been no need for such centers to have been built into the body. These sacred centers are like buttons on our outer garments (bodies) which button us close to the body of God. They are like closed eyes which we must open to see the glory of God; like gates which open into the Holy Temple, thru which we may enter into His everlasting life and joy; like conduits thru which His life, His love, His realization and power can flow to us for manifestation in our lives. This is the work to be accomplished in each heart and in humanity as a whole, namely, the *realization and manifestation of the presence* of the Christ.

Each Soul born into Earth life is a coal of fire, destined ultimately to be laid upon the altar of the Most High, either gladly thru his own recognition of the Light that lighteth everyone who cometh into the world, and swallowed up in the Love, giving up its life in eagerness to help serve and save humanity, or else, when purified thru suffering in many lives, after falling back like a dead cinder when it chose to glow and shine for itself alone, it finds its true place as a willing server of the Christ and humanity. Age after age have we tried and made some measure of advance. Age after age have we heard the call of the Christ: "Listen to the Voice of God! Listen to the little Voice that speaks within and obey. Respond to the Love which is Divine. Realize that God is Love: that there is no other God but the one God of Love. Thru Love is the advance of the Race brought about. Seek ye to find and manifest it truly."

In training children modern teachers have found it best not to emphasize their faults and threaten punishment, but to have them concentrate on that which is good and true and beautiful and constructive. And that is God's method. He tries to save His children from mistakes and their consequent suffering by having them realize the majesty and power of the Father, the beauty and Love of the Mother and the Light and Life of the Son. Instead of accusing them of their ignorance and their faults and pointing out His superiority, He not only illumines His chosen ones, but every 2,000 years He sends His only begotten Son — not a mortal — the Light of the World, down to Earth to mingle among the poorest and least learned — for they are of an open mind and a warm heart — to enlighten them and by His example show them how to climb the heights of spiritual attainment and step into the Chariot of Fire.

Since Nature, as a material expression of God, receives a new influx of life and power of expression in matter every Spring, there must also be higher and more spiritual expressions or outbreathings of God which also manifest periodically and cyclically. For, just as the rise of the Sun each Spring denotes the beginning of a new year in Nature, so does the rise of the Spiritual Sun every 2,000 years mark the beginning of a New Age for humanity: at this time the beginning of the great Aquarian Age. If we see the physical Sun rise from the southern hemisphere every Spring to pour out or sacrifice its life-force that the individual forms of life in Nature may have a renewed expression, we may well believe the world-old teaching that there is a Spiritual Sun which also rises periodically to bring to the spiritual life of humanity a period of renewed activity, growth and expression.

Today we stand on the brink of a new and wonderful manifestation, a new demonstration that God is Love, a Love so great that again He is to send to mankind an embodiment of the Cosmic Christos: is to send "his only begotten Son, that whosoever believeth in Him, should not perish, but have everlasting life. For God sent not his Son into the world to condemn the world; but that the world thru him might be saved."[3]

---

[3] *St John*, III, 16-17.

Today, as of old, once more are the heavens opened—our higher understanding—and the angels are broadcasting their joyous song to mankind. "Glory to God in the highest, and on Earth [and in the Earth and in the hearts of men—created in His image—be] peace, good will." Many advanced and illumined mortals may announce His coming and proclaim His message of Divine Love, but no mortal born of woman can be "He who is to come." For *the Son of God is not a mortal,* but the manifestation of a Divine and Celestial Being in human form: God Himself manifesting in the flesh.[4]

He can continue to come to mankind as He does today, unseen by man, and walk the streets and impress the minds of those who are capable of listening and responding, but He would do more. The day is dawning near when there must be a descent into physical manifestation, where He can demonstrate that *theophania* and *theopneusty*[5] or the manifestation of God to men is not merely an age-old teaching, attested to by the Initiates of all ages, but a practical fact and the most reasonable thing in the world, and following the universal Law of Manifestation[6] or the materialization of the invisible into the visible.

Those who seek the coming of the Son of God to mankind must realize that they must first awaken the

---

[4] For details see *Letters from the Teacher*, Vol. II, Curtiss, Chapter XIV.
[5] For details see *Realms of the Living Dead*, Curtiss, 13.
[6] Refer to *Chapter III*, herein.

Christ-consciousness in the cradle of their own hearts. And there must be at least a handful who can accomplish this without separating themselves from the world; for He must manifest in the world, and not merely in selected retreats far from the haunts of men, even though He may not walk the streets publicly. By remaining in the world we can form a Cup or Chalice, a Holy Grail, which can be so filled with the living presence of the Godhead that His only begotten Son can come to Earth in a Chariot of Fire and manifest to all the world for its enlightenment, comfort and salvation.

CHAPTER XIX

THE IMAGE OF GOD

"And God said, Let us make man in our image, after our likeness.... So God created man in his own image, in the image of God created he him; male and female created he them." *Genesis*, I, 26- 27.

"All things were made by him; and without him was not anything made that was made. In him was life; and the life was the light of men. And the light shineth in the darkness; and the darkness comprehended it not." *St. John*, I, 3-5.

"As we have borne the image of the earthy, we shall also bear the image of the heavenly." *I Corinthians*, XV, 49.

At this particular time we hear much about the so-called New Age, yet few realize that we have now entered into this new Aquarian Age. Nor do they understand the chief characteristics of this New Age and the mighty unfoldments it is destined to bring to both humanity and the planet. The chief characteristic of the New Age, as it turns a new page in the Book of Life, is that it ushers in a particular era of spiritual understanding, a new and greater comprehension of Divine Truth; the Age in which "there is nothing covered, that shall not be revealed; and hid, that shall not be known." Therefore, let us lay a foundation for this new understanding by going back to the beginning of things. For time is like a huge mill-wheel—the Mill of the Gods—forever turning round and round, and its movement men call the Flight of Time. As the planet is swept on into new regions in space, every revolution (Age) of this mighty Wheel of Time brings up some universal and world-old truth and grinds out or emphasizes some new aspect or understanding of it.

The farmer gathers the grain from what seemed before its cultivation and planting to be but barren ground, yet he scarcely gives a thought to the tremendous miracle by which the inert and inorganic soil is transmuted into food for man. Doubtless the Cave-man who first found grain good to eat was content to feed on the wild grain as he found it. But soon the advisability of crushing it was understood, and finally the mill-wheel, turning tirelessly round and round, was given the task of making it into flour as food for man. Similarly did the early Races of mankind assimilate their spiritual food direct from the Divine. But as the power of reason developed, direct cognition of Truth became so obscured by the rapidly developing intellect that only a remnant was left as intuition, so that the grain of spiritual Truth had to be ground ere man's intellect could understand and assimilate it.

In the beginning, when man was but a child, like an earthly father God saw that his needs were provided for, but when he became a man and was given free-will and personal responsibility he had to put away childish things and learn to provide for himself.

Thus in the mighty Mill of the Gods does the Wheel of Time—as illustrated in the zodiac—as cycles after cycles silently succeed each other, grind the grain of Truth finer and finer, at each turn making it more assimilable for our spiritual natures to feed upon. How truly did Jesus say: "I have meat to eat that ye know not of.... My meat is to do the will of Him that sent me, and to finish his work."[1] This is the food of which mankind knows so little, although it is made up of the vital grains of Truth which were given him in the beginning. And this spiritual "meat" man must some day find, eat and assimilate that he may build its strength and power into his character as spiritual growth.

As the Wheel slowly turns and generation succeeds generation, some there be who heed the turns of the Wheel and note that at each great revolution or Age the old truths and old ideas given mankind so long ago are being ground finer and finer, and new and mighty hidden aspects of them are being revealed as the old outer husks of material conceptions and interpretations, necessary, perhaps, in less enlightened ages, are being crushed and discarded and the fine flour of their inner meaning is being revealed for the spiritual nourishment of the humanity of the New Age. Thus do we gain a new concept of the truth back of the ancient poetic aphorism:

"Though the mills of God grind slowly, yet they grind exceeding small;

---
[1] *St. John*, IV, 32-4.

Though with patience He stands waiting, with exactness grinds He all."

As this mighty Wheel slowly begins its revolution for this New Age, let us examine the most fundamental teaching given us about man, *i.e.*, that God made man in His own image. And surely, as the Wheel turns and the Light of the Spiritual Sun illumines us with a new understanding, we will see the former grains of Truth arranging themselves into a new presentation of this fundamental idea. For no one who thinks seriously believes that the outer and physical form of man is the Image of God. Even so-called Super-man is far from being the Image of God, unless we reduce our idea of God to the anthropomorphic conception of but a magnified and glorified man.

An image is generally considered to be a more or less symbolic representation of some great truth or idea, fashioned and carved in such a way as to idealize some hidden or mystical truth or conception which those who study the image must think out and grasp. And it is this inner truth or Divine Reality, mystically hidden in man, that is the Image of God. This is equally true from Cave-man to Super-man.

This mysterious Image of God in man was fashioned as the crowning achievement of manifestation in this world of ours, which was created as a new field of action in which man, thru the learning of many new and most important lessons not possible on other planets, should learn to manifest that Image. Indeed,

THE IMAGE OF GOD

this Image was created male and female for this very purpose. As the Light of Intuition illumines this idea we should stop and think why such emphasis was placed upon this point; for the fact of sex would not be so emphasized were it not a fundamental feature, and the greatest of all lessons, man came to this planet to work out and learn.

In the higher spiritual realms both the masculine and feminine aspects of the Image (Soul) were contained unseparated within the one spiritual, egg-shaped aura. But when the time came for this spiritual Image to descend into and manifest in matter it had to have an instrument formed out of the substance or "dust" of the Earth thru which to contact and function on Earth. And when fully materialized, this form had to come under the law of the physical plane, the Law of Duality, and manifest in separate organisms, male and female. Hence it has taken the Divine Image countless ages and innumerable incarnations to evolve a body that could even partially yet progressively express ever new and higher aspects of the Image or Spiritual Self. For, like the Earth itself, the body, while a beautiful and wondrous mechanism, was not and still is not, a perfected and finished product. Even yet, after all these ages of evolution, man has as many hidden mysteries to unfold within himself as has the Earth within itself. And the Earth reveals her mysteries to man only as he develops the capacity to understand, and learns the corresponding lessons within himself.

In the early stages of spiritual unfoldment this Image of God is like a babe wrapped in swaddling clothes, yet predestined to manifest in and thru man, making him "as one of us, knowing good and evil." As the masculine and feminine types of mind look at things from different angles, each must create after his or her own way of thinking their individual realization of the Image of God within and strive to bring it forth in their lives.

As the Wheel of Time grinds on it finds much chaff and, from the hopperful of certain periods, seemingly little flour, yet even the chaff is the outer husk of the grain. And as the chaff, when spread upon the ground or when reduced to ashes, helps to fertilize the ground, so with the chaff ground out in man's evolution. Those who cannot and will not accept and follow the laws of spiritual growth and unfoldment, and those who persist in evil—opposition to the Law—as the Wheel of Life grinds on are ground out as the chaff of humanity from those who represent the flour, because the latter are striving to work with the Law, helping make smooth the way of understanding and helping to feed mankind with spiritual food. In other words, with the ushering in of this new Aquarian Age the time has come when those who are spiritually unevolved and those who refuse to work with God's Law in spite of all the teachings and helps which God has given them, will not be permitted to incarnate again until those who are advanced and faithful to the Law have had an opportunity to reach a certain advanced stage of spiritual unfoldment, unhampered by the undeveloped and slothful ones. The latter, however, are not neglected, but for a certain cycle remain in other realms, much as incorrigible children might be shut away from their law-abiding companions in a special school or reformatory until they had learned the needed lessons.

Altho man brings much inharmony and evil into the world, thru his misuse of the materials and forces created by God which man should use to fashion an Eden of peace and harmony, nevertheless all inharmony and evil is but temporary; is but the irritating chaff which must be separated from the flour, for only that which is in harmony with Divine Law can endure. What could be a plainer answer to the oft-repeated question that since we can conceive of God as creating only good, how came evil into the world? God spake the word and created a world of beauty and harmony because He spake according to the laws of beauty and harmony. Man also speaks words which are creating his world, not only his world within, but his general atmosphere, his conditions in life and his environment. And he has to live in that world of his own creation. If his words have not been constructive, if they have not been spoken according to the laws of beauty and harmony, then he finds himself living in a world of self-created inharmony which he calls evil. And he must suffer in his self-made world of inharmony until he learns how to create his true world of beauty and harmony.

The very fact that man can create such a world is proof that man is created in the Image of God with the God-given power to create a world of beauty, harmony and joy if he will. And he must keep on incarnating again and again and reaping the results of his creations until he learns to create in the Image of God and not in the image of man.

But if man has created all the evil, sin, sickness and death from which he suffers, how did he get the power to do so? As a son of God, created in His Image, he has as much power as the Wheel has to grind the flour from out the golden grain and cast the chaff aside. And as the chaff can be utilized either to bring forth better crops or can be piled in a useless or harmful heap, so with man's mistakes and evil creations. They can be turned to good if he learns the lessons from the suffering which they bring or they can accumulate as a great burden which hampers his evolution until consumed by the Fire of the Law as the karmic suffering which he must reap, both for himself and for the world into which he has sent it forth and whose aura he has tainted with such creations. But out of the ashes of such experiences, in humility and sorrow, will he gradually bring forth a better and higher understanding of Divine Law and the Divine Love which is back of seemingly stern exact justice.

At present that Divine Life which pours thru us from the Image of God within, and which St. John tells us is "the light of men,"[2] is the true Spiritual

---

[2] *St. John*, I.

Light which, altho shining within each Soul born into the world, is obscured by the darkness of man's inharmony, selfishness, disobedience and wrong thinking, and "the darkness comprehended it not." Nevertheless, the "life that is the light of men" is still shining in every heart. But only as man believes this and asks for help to comprehend and utilize it can the darkness which hides the Light, like a dense, chilling fog, be dispelled. The *Bible* sets forth the fundamental truths concerning the Image of God and its Light, and God has given to man the light of reason with which it is his duty to analyze, understand, and make use of these truths for himself and all the world, and not cry out for God to do it for him. For, since each Soul has the "life that is the light of men," each has at least a spark of understanding which it is his privilege and duty to fan and expand into a steady glowing Light which shall illumine his pathway thru life. Hence man has the power to dissipate the darkness if he will and create a new world for himself.

But, alas, many cry out that the darkness grows blacker and more dense the more they strive. How can they see and comprehend, since they were born into such hampering and limiting Earth conditions? We must remember that this darkness and these hampering conditions are the result of our lack of accomplishment in this and past lives during which we created darkness rather than Light. We find ourselves in such conditions not as a punishment, but as the best conditions in which to learn our lessons and unfold the lacking qualities and powers necessary to manifest the Image of God. For if we will not learn by precept we must learn by experience. If we refuse to follow the Divine Law, as set forth by the Great Teachers of all ages, we must be allowed to find out for ourselves that unless we use God's gifts as they were intended to be used we will bring only disappointment, sorrow and suffering upon ourselves. This Divine Life can manifest either as a radiant Light leading us onward and upward or as a fire consuming the chaff which we have neglected or refused to dispose of or upon which we are trying to feed instead of the flour; for we must all reap the results of our own creations.

Many have sat down beside the chaff, as the mighty Wheel grinds out the golden grain, and wondered at the darkness caused by the dust of its continual showers. Many have made their abiding place in the chaff, which they call worldly success or pleasure or self-aggrandizement or wealth, because the flakes of chaff have a golden glitter as they float for the moment in the sunshine as they fall to earth. But when the world they have built for themselves from the chaff grows old and mouldy, or when the storms beat upon it and it dissolves in a viscid mass about them and engulfs them, they bitterly bewail their fate and cry out that there can be no Image of God within, no Divine Law or Divine Love, or their world would not be allowed to get in such a condition. But they forget that while the substance of the outer conditions (the chaff) was created by God and should be used to fertilize their growth and make pleasant and comfortable and happy their sojourn here on Earth, it was not made for their permanent abiding place.

While we must live in the world we must not identify ourselves with it or allow it and its concerns to occupy the supreme place in our consciousness and life. We should endeavor to use all things and conditions for His glory, to bring forth the Image of God that is within us and allow it to manifest and illumine our lives. We must never blame God for our limitations or our failures, for we alone are to blame. Once we realize this fundamental truth we can begin consciously to redeem our failures and overcome our limitations by seeking to let the Light of the Image shine forth; for as long as we have life we have the Light of God and His power of creativeness within us.

Since this Image of God is not only the Light of men, but is also the source of our physical life, it has built into our very flesh centers or avenues for the manifestation of all the God-powers and possibilities which we inherit as Sons of God. He has given us a mind with the power of reaching up to the God-consciousness, as well as to regulate wisely all the affairs of our outer life toward the ultimate outshining of His Image. Like the triple Light from which it sprang and like the triple light of the Earth—Sun, Moon and stars—this mind of ours is three-fold in its aspects:[3] the Super-conscious (Sun), Rational (stars), and Sub-conscious (Moon) mind. God also created man with many other centers of expression, each of which is three-fold in its nature: one aspect to rule the physical and bring about peace, harmony and perfect health and happiness: one to bring him into conscious touch with the Divine, and one to radiate the Light, Life and Power of the Image within. Thus is man a trinity of Light which is capable of so manifesting in his life as to be "a lamp unto my feet, and a light unto my path," the Path of Illumination and Attainment.

How are we to gain this unfoldment and illumination? Not by laboriously practicing various exercises which are said to unfold centers which the vast majority of persons are not ready to develop and whose untimely stimulation in the unprepared presents grave dangers, but by seeking to find and correlate with the Image of God within, the Christ within our hearts, and cultivate and radiate all that pertains to that heart center, and thus create a world wherein love and the Christ-power shall dominate. For have we not been told: "Seek ye first the kingdom of God and his righteousness, and all these things shall be added unto you"?

Only as we learn to recognize the Christ which is our life, our light and our guide, can we begin to manifest the Image of God which is our Real, Divine

---

[3] For a full exposition see *The Key to the Universe*, Curtiss, 259-62.

Self. This can be accomplished, first by going directly to Him in prayer and aspiration and asking[4] daily and hourly for His guidance and help, and for a realization of the truth of the axiom, "As a man thinketh in his *heart* so is he." But it must be a realization of the heart—a realization which nothing can disturb, and not mere affirmations of the head—a realization of the Image of God within.

The second step is, thru His guidance and power, to curb, control and, without despising, wisely use all the physical centers, faculties and functions, realizing that in their perfect functioning and wise use we are obeying the will of God who created them to aid us in manifesting His Image. For as they are dominated, controlled and used in a natural, normal and pure manner, their corresponding spiritual aspects will, in due time, grow, develop and function normally without being forced thru direct concentration upon them. The most rapid method of aiding this development is to learn to express love, not love fashioned after man's conception—love of possession, love of power, love of self-indulgence, etc.,—for that holds within it the very darkness—selfishness, lust, jealousy, greed, etc.,—which real Love is meant to vanquish. It is Divine Love we must learn to understand and express if we are to banish the darkness from our lives.

Only as we keep our minds and hearts fixed on the idea that the end to be achieved is conscious union

---

[4] The *Prayer for Light* and the *Prayer to the Divine Indweller* are great helps.

with God, and tread the path in a normal but inspired way, guided by the Light from His Image, can we show by our lives how blessed is the Way, the Truth and the Life. Thus can we lead others into the fullness of the outshining of that Light and help them to manifest the Image that is within them. The same laws and processes we see exemplified in Nature, when the Sun rises after a night of darkness and when Spring follows a desolate and bitter winter, are fulfilled in ourselves. But we can hasten or retard the dawn of the New Day and the coming of our spiritual Springtime according to our response or lack of response to that Divine Life which is the Light of men and the resulting manifestation of the Image of God.

CHAPTER XX

EMMANUEL

"Behold a virgin shall be with child, and shall bring forth a son, and they shall call his name Emmanuel, which being interpreted is, God with us." *St. Matthew*, I, 23.

In these momentous times each awakened personality, and the very Age itself, is passing through a period when wonderful prophecies are being fulfilled. Altho allegorically described in the *Bible*, ere this Aquarian Age has turned many pages of its life history, many of the prophecies are destined to be actually fulfilled.

As applied to himself the mystic interprets the story of Jesus' life as set forth in the Gospels as an allegory explaining the birth of the Christ-consciousness in each heart when the proper stage of Soul-unfoldment is reached, and the various stages of its manifestation until the at-one-ment with the Father-in-heaven is attained. It is this emanation of Divinity which lies buried in the mystical heart-center of each human being, like a seed in the ground, that must be quickened and awakened from its dormant state by every virgin heart, that is, by every heart that has been purified and made ready for this mystical birth.

This law is illustrated in the passage, "The Holy

Ghost shall come upon thee, and the power of the Highest shall overshadow thee: therefore also that holy thing which shall be born of thee shall be called the Son of God."[1] Following out the old medieval idea of there being something impure in sex, many students have thought that this passage indicated that there must be some mysterious way whereby a physical child could be generated without the use of the sex function. But since a physical body cannot be generated without a physical father it is evident that this passage cannot refer to the generation of a physical body, but symbolizes the birth of the Christ-consciousness in the heart—symbolized by Mary—of all who have reached the stage of spiritual unfoldment where they can listen to the inner Voice and respond to the overshadowing of the Holy Ghost (Mother) and "the power of the Highest" (Father).[2]

The word translated virgin is *almah*, whose root meaning is "hidden, secret, to conceal." As used in the text it refers to "one who has never been seen by man." Mystically interpreted the verse quoted at the head of this chapter means, Behold, almah or that which is concealed, hidden, secret and never seen by man, shall have a new conception and bring forth a new and positive (male) manifestation of God within us. The new manifestation is brought forth in the concealed mystery-chamber of the spiritual heart where the Holy Ghost and the Power of the Highest

---

[1] *St. Luke*, II, 35.
[2] See lesson *The Immaculate Conception*, Curtiss.

shall unite to bring forth this new spiritual child whose name shall be called Emmanuel or God-within-us.

Altho this passage is usually connected with the birth of Jesus, it is not properly so connected, for nowhere in the *Bible* was He ever called Emmanuel. The prophecy was an announcement of the inevitable result of the downpouring of the mighty Christ-force into the heart that has become virgin pure. The name Emmanuel therefore refers to the birth of the Christ-consciousness within each heart, while the name Jesus refers to the manifestation to the world of that Divine Consciousness which is phenomenally embodied in each Age in the person of the Avatar.[3]

In medieval days it was taught that to worship God in heaven it was necessary to starve and mortify the body and degrade as a tempter the God within. Those misguided ones who followed that doctrine were thus working directly against bringing forth the Emmanuel within them. But as the sweep of cosmic cycles brings us closer to a realization of what the New Age contains for us, and the few who have made their hearts virgin pure see the Sign of the Son of Man in heaven and the water-pot of Aquarius pouring out the mystic Water of Life upon humanity, their vision is illumined, and within their longing hearts they feel the stirring of a new life, like a babe quickening in its mother's womb. They feel it struggling to cast off the hampering swaddling clothes of the outer conscious-

---

[3] See "The Doctrine of Avatara," in *The Voice of Isis*, Curtiss, Chapter X.

ness, of misconception and misunderstanding. For when they listen in the Silence they seem to hear a tiny voice whispering: "I am the living Christ-seed planted in your heart. But I can grow only as you nourish me with your attention and water me with Divine Love. I am divine even as my Father-in-heaven is divine, and my presence makes you divine. I am immortal and my life within you will make you immortal if you 'feed on me in your heart with prayer and thanksgiving.'"

All who would bring forth this wonderful child Emmanuel so long hidden within must seek Him so earnestly and desire Him so ardently that the mystical centers in which He dwells will be penetrated by and so filled with aspiration and Christ-love that He will be awakened from His long sleep. Then they will be so filled with the overwhelming desire to find Him and serve Him that all their faculties—the disciples—are ready to leave all and follow Him. Thus will these centers be stimulated and quickened and His growth promoted.

Nothing anyone can do or say can help us to know Him. No matter how illumined a teacher may be he can only tell us *about* Emmanuel. To *know* Him for ourselves He must be born within us and we must correlate with Him, bring our problems to Him and let Him guide our lives. It may be that we are born with a strong sense of duty—brought over from a past life—to certain people or to a certain cause. And this may tend to make us reluctant to cope with the duties confronting us today. But we can safely leave the adjustment of past Karma in the hands of the Lords of Karma, knowing that they will inevitably find a way for us to fulfill it. Often we fulfill it unconsciously by our readiness to take up the duty that lies nearest.

Holding on to some fancied duty of the past only makes our burden heavier, while doing the duty that is plainly set before us in the present will lift the burden and leave us free to take new steps onward. If we believe that we should hold back from some positive duty confronting us in this life because of some unfulfilled duty or unlearned lesson of the past, we should remember that the present day duties are ours because of that past, hence the past duties can best be worked out by resolutely fulfilling those of the present.

A still greater mistake is to hold on to any old idea, thought, habit or seeming duty that is hampering to the growth and manifestation of the newly awakened Christ-consciousness within. This is one of the most important decisions life holds for us, and one which each awakened Soul must decide for himself. For many almost fear to believe that they have felt the stir of the Christ within their hearts; that they have seen His light or heard His voice or felt the warmth of His love within them. Yet we can always recognize the inner guidance if we seek it, for with the development of intuition and later the opening of our mystic centers there comes a surety, a calm conviction which quiets all doubts, even though we may not be unfolded enough to hear the Inner Voice.

This newly revealed spiritual consciousness or Emmanuel gives to the entire body a new vibration, and often a new sensation of glowing warmth, a new power of endurance, a new realization that we are not alone, nor weak, nor ignorant. We realize that the "Divinity that shapes our ends" has been found, and that with its help we can consciously shape our own ends. Like the Wise Men of the *Bible* story we may have long since seen His star in the East and have journeyed, footsore and weary, o'er moor and fen, o'er mountain crag and trackless desert, yet when we have found and recognized and worshipped Him and have laid the gifts of all our talents at His feet, we must then return to our own country. In other words, *realization alone is not enough.* From the country of that realization—the far country from which we set out upon our search—we must bring back into our daily lives the glow of the living fire of Divinity. We must let the power and consciousness of Emmanuel fill our hearts, our minds, our bodies and manifest in our lives as a new ability to understand life and our fellowmen, a new power to accomplish His will in every-day affairs.

Yet having thus brought forth Emmanuel into the affairs of the outer world we must be careful not to call attention to Him, not to boast or point to our newly acquired realization and powers, lest the Herod of a skeptical world, or the Herod of our old habits of thought and life, slay the young child. In fact, He must remain hidden and unheralded until He is mystically twelve years of age.[4] Then He will be able to meet all the doctors in the temple or all the reason and logic of our minds and not only protect Himself but astonish them with His wisdom.

The realization of this new fount of life, love and power of Emmanuel within us is the true interpretation of that old revival hymn now so widely condemned as cannibalistic.

> "There is a fountain filled with blood
> Drawn from Emmanuel's veins.
> And sinners plunged beneath that flood
> Lose all their guilty stains."

For since the blood is the carrier of the life-force of the body it is used to symbolize the spiritual life-force of the Christ. And since the heart is the source of that fountain of blood, the heart is the center in which Emmanuel, the source of the God-within-us, is to be found. In fact, the true spiritual heart is the cradle in which the Christ-consciousness is born.

One of the vital differences between man and the lower animals is that man possesses certain centers which are only embryonic in the animals. In the majority of humanity these mystic centers are but little developed, hence their functions and possibilities are scarcely suspected. Especially is this true of the heart-center. For while the chief function of the physical heart is to pump the blood through the body and

---
[4] For explanation see *The Key of Destiny*, Curtiss, 54.

keep its physical life force flowing, the spiritual heart is the center through which man contacts the cosmic current of the living Christ-force and keeps it flowing through him. Only as we cultivate this center and let the Christ-force flow through us unimpeded can we unfold our other centers one by one until we become the Lord of Creation and fulfill the mandate given us when man began his cycle of evolution on this planet: "Be fruitful, and multiply, and replenish the earth, and subdue it; and have dominion over the fish of the sea, and over the fowl of the air, and over every living thing that moveth upon the earth."

The body of man is indeed a marvelous creation, but man himself must find the key which will unlock the mysterious inner chamber wherein Emmanuel, the God-within-us, lies hidden. Today many are striving to unfold these mystic centers through various physical exercises and yoga practices, but until Emmanuel is born within the heart such development as may result can only open the consciousness to the astral world,[5] not to the spiritual world. Such an opening to the astral world not only stimulates all our faculties and tendencies, both good and evil, but as it opens new avenues of consciousness it also subjects us to terrible forces and temptations from the astral. And unless Emmanuel has already been born and begun to rule within us we are likely to be swept away into terrible conditions of both body and mind, often to complete mental and physical breakdown, just as the pregnant

---

[5] For details see *Realms of the Living Dead*, Curtiss.

mother who does not correlate with the incarnating Soul is often swept into the currents of inharmony caused by the conflict of the many undeveloped Souls who are fighting for incarnation through her, even to the point of causing what is termed puerperal insanity. Never forget that the love and wise guidance of Emmanuel who lovingly waits within must first be unfolded if we are to unfold the other centers constructively and safely and grow as the flower grows.

Through aspiration, realization, understanding and devotion we must find Emmanuel and, one by one in sacred awe, unwrap the swaddling bands of misconception which hide Him from our sight and manifest Him in our lives. To do this we must understand that God is just as truly within us here and now as it is true that the life-force is in the blood here and now. And just as the life-force, altho unseen and often unrecognized, yet potently manifests in the blood to bring us health, strength, vitality and the power to manifest physical life, just as surely does the inner spiritual life-force of Emmanuel, altho unseen and unrecognized, flow through us, giving us comfort, guidance, strength and the power to manifest our spiritual life.

From the heart that is spiritually unfolded there goes forth a golden radiance which shines like the fabled pot of gold at the end of the rainbow. Like children we hear about, and often dream of finding this pot of gold, but, alas, we know not how or where to look. It looks so close, yet when we start out to find it the journey seems endless. But if we have faith and follow our inner guidance and keep our mind's eye fixed upon the spiritual rainbow, the reflection of the color rays produced by the shining of the Sun of God on our tears as we look up to Him after a storm, we will realize that all its wondrous colors come from God or are reflected from the pot of gold within our hearts, even tho we may see the colors only after a storm. Some day we will find the pot of gold, not afar off at the other end of the rainbow, but within us, as Emmanuel, the greatest gift of God to man.

PRAYERS

Prayers of *The Order of Christian Mystics*

PRAYER FOR LIGHT
O Christ! Light Thou within my heart
The Flame of Divine Love and Wisdom,
That I may dwell forever in the radiance of Thy
   countenance
And rest in the Light of Thy smile!

MORNING PRAYER
I have within me the power of the Christ!
I can conquer all that comes to me today!
I am strong enough to bear every trial
And accept every joy
And to say
Thy will be done!

HEALING PRAYER
O thou loving and helpful Master Jesus!
Thou who gavest to Thy disciples power to heal the sick!
We, recognizing Thee, and realizing Thy divine Presence
   with us,
Ask Thee to lay Thy hands (powers) upon us in healing
   Love.
Cleanse US from all OUR sins, and by the divine power of
   Omnipotent Life,
Drive out the atoms of inharmony and disease, and
Fill our bodies full to overflowing with Life and Love and
   Purity.

PRAYER OF PROTECTION
O Christ! Surround and fill me and Thy Order with the
   Flame of Divine Love and Wisdom, That it may purify,
   illumine and guide us in all things.
May its Spiritual Fire form a rampart of Living Flame
   around me and Thy Order,
To protect us from all harm.
May it radiate to every heart, consuming all evil and
   intensifying all good.
In the name of the Living Christ! Amen.

PRAYER OF DEMONSTRATION
    I am a child of the Living God!
    I have within me the all-creating power of the Christ!
    It radiates from me and blesses all I contact.
    It is my Health, my Strength, my Courage,
    My Patience, my Peace, my Poise,
    My Power, my Wisdom, my Understanding,
    My Joy, my Inspiration, and my Abundant Supply.
    Unto this great Power I entrust all my problems,
    Knowing they will be solved in Love and Justice.
    (Mention all problems connected with your worldly affairs,
        visualize each and conclude with the following words)
    O Lord Christ! I have laid upon Thy altar all my wants and
        desires.
    I know Thy Love, Thy Wisdom, Thy Power and Thy
        Graciousness.
    In Thee I peacefully rest knowing that all is well.
    For Thy will is my will. Amen.

PRAYER TO THE DIVINE INDWELLER
    Come, O Lord of Life and Love and Beauty!
    Thou who art myself and yet art God!
    And dwell in this body of flesh,
    Radiating all the beauty of holiness and perfection,
    That the flesh may out-picture all that Thou art within!
    Even so, come, O Lord. Amen.

PRAYER TO THE DIVINE MOTHER
    O Divine Mother!
    Illumine me with Divine Wisdom,
    Vivify me with Divine Life and
    Purify me with Divine Love,
    That in all I think and say and do
    I may be more and more Thy child. Amen.

GRACE BEFORE MEALS
    I am a creator.
    By the power of my spiritualized Will
    I consciously gather all the forces from this food,
    And use them to create health, strength and harmony
    In all my bodies (physical, astral and mental).

PRAYERS

PRAYER OF DEVOTION

We, Thy chosen servants, to whom Thou hast given the great privilege of becoming co-workers with the Masters of Wisdom, ask that we may have Wisdom and Power and Courage and Humility to carry us through the work of this day.

We open our hearts that the Divine Love of the Master may fill us; that all irritation, inharmony and slothfulness may be transmuted into Love that shall draw us closer in unity to all our fellow workers both seen and unseen; that we may grow absolutely one with the force of Wisdom and Compassion that is sent forth to accomplish the great work for humanity.

Give us all things necessary, that there may be no hampering conditions.

Lead us through this day, in the name of the Divine, Ever-living Christ, that the will of the Father may be done in us and through us forevermore. Amen.

PRAYER FOR WORLD HARMONY

Glory and honor and worship be unto Thee, O Lord Christ, Thou who art the Life and Light of all mankind.

Thou art the King of Glory to whom all the peoples of the Earth should give joyful allegiance and service.

Inspire mankind with a realization of true Brotherhood.

Teach us the wisdom of peace, harmony and co-operation.

Breathe into our hearts the understanding that only as we see ourselves as parts of the one body of humanity can peace, harmony, success and plenty descend upon us.

Help us to conquer all manifestations of inharmony and evil in ourselves and in the world.

May all persons and classes and nations cease their conflicts, and unselfishly strive for peace and good-will that the days of tribulation may be shortened.

Bless us all with the radiance of Thy Divine Love and Wisdom that we may ever worship Thee in the beauty of holiness.

In the Name of the Living Christ we ask it. Amen.

PRAYER FOR THE CHRIST POWER

O Lord Christ! Thou who hast planted within me
The Immortal Power of Spiritual Love and Life,

Help me so to correlate with Thy divine overshadowing
   Presence,
That all hampering conditions shall be swallowed up
In the Light of the Living Christ Power. Amen.

Evening Prayer
   As the physical Sun
   Disappears from our sight
   May the Spiritual Sun
   Arise in our hearts,
   Illumine our minds
   And shed its radiant blessing
   Upon all we contact

INDEX

A

Acorn, 35
Adam, and Eve, Chapter viii, 81; androgynous, 83, 109; expelled, 131, 140; names animals, 94, 104; not historical,82; the first, 50, 67; the second, 55-6, 83
Affinities, 162
Agassiz, Prof., quoted, 33
Age, the Aquarian, 215-16
Ages, the Dark, 120-7, 206
Alkalescence, need of, 38
Almah, meaning of, 230
Animals, Adam names, 94, 104
Ape, body like an, 84
Apple, of discord, 91
Aquarius, symbol of, 231
Armageddon, battle of, 123
Atlantosauris, 102
Augustine, St., quoted, 96-7, 109
Aulde, Dr. John, quoted, 39
Aura, the, 219
Avatar, the, 181, 23

B

Bara, meaning of, 54
Beginning, word for, 36
Beguiled, word for, 130
Behaviorism, 105
Belly, crawling on, 137-8
Be-rashith, meaning of, 36
Bible, allegorical, 112-13; no conflict with, xi, 65
Binet, Prof., quoted, 37
Biology, teaches, 19
Black Boy, 22
Blood, symbol of the, 235-6-7
Body, animal, 56-9; ape-like, 84; centers in, 111, 206; defective, 67-9, 70; essential, 56; evolving, 49, 66-9, 169; formed, 52; instincts of, 102; not despise, 206; the spiritual, 66-8, 75
Bose, Sir C., quoted, 41
Brahmadanda, 133
Brains, function of the, 31
Brass, 127, 132
Breath, of Life, 56
Buddha, 183
Bushman, 22
Buttons, simile of, 210

C

Caduceus, 133
Cain, 80, 131
Calcium, need of, 39
Causes, invisible, 34; seed, 142
Centers, open normally, 139, 206-7, 236
Chaff, simile of, 221-4
Change, progress requires, 75
Chariot, Swing Low, Sweet, 189, 197, 211-12; cycles of, 190-5
Chemic Problem in Nutrition, quoted, 39
Chemotaxis, 38
Children of the New Age, 155
Christ, consciousness, 205, 231; force, 77, 206; not a mortal, 213; seed, 203
Christos, The, 181-4; Chapter xviii, 201; return of, 212-13
Claims, 199
Coal, each Soul a, 210-11
Collier's, quoted, 17, 25-7

Coming, the Second, 212-13
Coming World Changes, quoted, 79, 190
Complex, inferiority, 92
Compte de Gabalis, quoted, 175-9, 184
Consciousness, Christ, 205, 231; cosmic, 55, 168; kinds of, 37; of cells, 37; of plants, 41; self-, 85, 118; Super-, 43; vast, 32
Creation, 44, 54, 119; accounts of, 55; days of, 63-4; Hierarchies of, 119; Manifesting the, Chapters vi-vii, 66-74
Creations, constructive, 78-9, 123; destructive, 78, 122; God's, 49, 55, 121; man's, 49, 72, 121-2, 221-2
Creators, two, 121
Creeds, man-made, xiv, xv, 79, 180; Nicene, 202
Cross, 134-5
Crucifixion, 68, 134-5
Currents, short-circuited, 157
Curse, of serpent, 136-7
Cycles, of Chariot, 190-5; planetary, 186

D

Days, of creation, 63-4
Determinism, 105
Devaki, 182
Dinosaur, 102
Disease, cause of, 122, 158
Divorce, Jesus and, 152; necessary, 153-4
Duality, Law of, 83, 150, 169, 219; not multiplicity, 165
Dust, contents of, 102-3
Duty, 233
Dynamism, doctrine of, 31

E

East, symbol of, 98, 100
Eden, contents of, 106-7; expelled from, 131; *Garden in*, Chapter ix, 94; located, 77, 140; meaning of, 109; trees in, 109
Eggs, human, 86
Elijah, 191
Elisha, 191
Embryo, human, 19, 20-1, 42; of whale, 20
Embryology, teaches, 19
Emmanuel, Chapter xx, 229; realize, 234-7
Encyclopedia Britannica, quoted, 17, 25
Energy, doctrine of, 31
Environment, effect of, 43-5; surmounted, 106
Epidemics, cause of, 122
Evil, good from, 120; meaning of, 116; origin of, 221
Evolution, hypothesis only, 23; Law of, 169; new stage of, 72; not complete, 47, 66; not mechanical, 22, 36, 171; progressive, 27, 45, 176; time of, 46
Exercises, not necessary, 207, 226, 236
Eye, the Third, 116

F

Facts, interpretation of, xiv
Fall, before sex, 61; of man, 60-1
Fertilization, 41
Fire, Chariot of, 189; necessary, 178; of the Lord, 191-2-4
Flame, simile of, 180
Forum, The, quoted, 113
Fossils, 20-1
Freedom, no absolute, 162; of sex, 163
Frigid, 157-8
From the Unconscious to the Conscious, quoted, 23-5, 31-3-6, 42, 54-5, 66
Functions, "mere animal," 148
Fundamentalists, right, xv, 49, 55

G

Garden, banished from, 140; in Eden, Chapter ix, 94; meaning of, 110; re-enter, 141
Gardener, the Great, 68
Gardner, Helen, 88
Gems of Mysticism, quoted, 77
Geology, blanks in records, 21
Ghost, the Holy, 182, 230
Gill-slits, 19
Gland, the Pineal, 116, 124
God, 32, 175; Chapters xvi, xvii, xviii, 201; *Image of*, Chapter xix, 215; 67, 200-5-18; Fire as, 177; is Love, 186; pre-Christian, 96-7, 179; Son of, 81-4, 202-3; the Father, 175, 184; the Mother, 189; threefold, 175; unjust, 113
Gold, pot of, 237
Good, all not, 120
Grail, the Holy, 188, 214
Growth, why it stops, 35

H

Heathen, 179, 180
Heaven, come from, 59; old idea of, 198; opened, 213
Hell, 120-1
Herb, of field, 48
Hierarchies, creative, 44, 119
Higher Self, 153
Horse, evolution of, 21
Huxley, Prof., quoted, 17

I

Ida, 133
Ideation, Divine, 55
Image of God, Chapter xix, 215; 49, 67, 73
Immortality, in the flesh, 140
Incarnation, method of, 129; of ideals, 90; of Spirit, 58; Souls seeking, 90
Indweller, the Divine, 74-54
Inheritance, 73, 40-1-5

Initiator, the Great, 114
Instincts, 102-8; superseded, 118
Intuition, rôle of, 104
Involution, 42, 67, 83
Isis, 182

J

Jesus, life symbolic, 229; on divorce, 152

K

Kabbalah Unveiled, The, quoted, 150
Karma, brother and sister, 61; race, 142-3; reap our, 71, 142-3; what is, 197; world, 68
Keith, Sir Arthur, quoted, 23
Key of Destiny, The, quoted, 235
Key to the Universe, quoted, 97, 146-8, 150-1-3, 163-6, 226
Kidney, cells of, 37
Kingdom, fifth, 56; fourth, 56
Kingsland, Anna B., quoted, 142
Knowledge, Tree of, 114
Krishna, 183
Kundalini, force, 116, 131-2-3; in brain, 134

L

Landone, Brown, quoted, 36, 51-4-5, 81, 110-16, 127, 170
Lethe, Cup of, 114
Letters from the Teacher, Vol. ii, quoted, 203, 213
Life, not explained, 27; River of, 112; Tree of, xiii, 91, 112-4, 123, 140, 164
Light, the Prayer for, 188
Lincoln, Abraham, example of, 106
Lodge, Sir Oliver, quoted, 28, 44, 120
Loeb, Dr., quoted, 43
Logography, 104
Love, devastating, 193; God is, 160; higher, 160

M

Magnesium, infiltration, 39
Man, banished, 122; Spiritual, 50-1-2, 82, 118; Super-, 117
Manger, 207
Manifestation, Law of, Chapter iii, 33, 49
Marriage, authorities on, 164; from the beginning, 151; group, 164; highest state, 154; in heaven, 151, 160-1, 170 ; man-made, 160; of brother and sister, 161; object of, 154, 170; spiritual, 170; trial, 164; true, 151-160
Materialism, absurd, 29; bankrupt, 28; limited, 25-6; out of date, 29
Mates, complementary, 36-7, 152, 162; from the beginning, 151; not incarnated, 161; spiritual, 151; union of, 156
Message of Aquaria, The, quoted, xiii, 46, 58, 61, 75-7, 82, 96, 107, 168
Millikan, Prof. Robert A., quoted, xi, 17, 25-7-8-9
Mind, above brain, 31; Divine, 32, 78; effect of, 85, 107; intuitive, 88; not all, 31; plastic, xiii; rational, 88; use of, 117
Monsters, 85
Morality, necessity for, 113
Mother, the Divine, 70, 182
Mother India, quoted, 132-7

N

Nachash, 127, 130
Nasha, 130
Nature, book of, 142
Noah, 104
Nod, land of, 81

O

Oracles, Sibylline, 175-9
Organs, vestigial, 20

Origins, not explained, 28, 45
Osmosis, 37
Ouspensky, Prof., quoted, 26, 30, 66, 73-4
Over-Soul, 42

P

Paraclete, 181
Pattern, Inner, in Bible, 48; necessity of a, 30-3, 49, 65; not in seed, 69
Perfect Way, The, quoted, 142
Personality, 119
Pingala, 33
Plan, predestined, 22, 46, 168, 176
Prayer, For Light, Evening, Divine Mother, 188
Progress, change to, 75; not uniform, 22-3
Promiscuity, 152, unsatisfactory, 156
Psychic Life of Micro-organisms, quoted, 37

R

Race, salvation of the, 129
Races, besides Adam, 81; the early, 84
Radium, 77-8
Rainbow, simile of, 237-8
Realms of the Living Dead, quoted, 134, 213, 236
Rib, symbology of, 87-9, 90
River of Life, 112
Rivers, of Eden, 97-8, 100-1
Rod, of Moses, 133-7; of power, 141
Rome, 165

S

Sacrifice, Law of, 61, 162
Samson, 80
Satisfaction, Law of, 155-6
School, Elohistic, 52; Jehovistic, 53

Science, achievements of, 18; limits of, 26
Secret Doctrine, The, quoted, 33, 44, 60, 81-5, 94, 115, 128
Seed, no pattern in, 68
Self, Higher, A and B, 153; Real, 69
Serpent, cursed, 136; force, 116, 125; meaning of, 114, 126, 130-6; not evil, 125; not sex, 27; *Power*, Chapters xi, xii, 125, 136
Seventh Seal, The, quoted, 33, 74, 142
Sex, aim of, 159, 160; blessed, 128-9; divine, 146-7-8; equality, 163; in Soul, 88; -force, creative, 119; -force, short circuited, 157; not evil, 157; outgrown, 156; procreative, 147; satisfaction, 155-6
Sexes, separation of, 84
Shekinah, 191-6
Sibyls, 184
Sin, original, 62-3
Soul, a living, 56; as a cell, 43; each a coal, 210-11
Souls, seeking incarnation, 90
St. Paul, quoted, 59, 60
Summary, Chapter xv, 168
Sun, behind the Sun, 190; Spiritual, 203
Super-man, 117
Supplement, Chapters xvi to xx, 174
Sword, the Flaming, 123, 134

T

Taft, Ex-President Wm, H., quoted, 24
Tears, 76
Temptation, 131
Tertium Organum, quoted, 26, 30, 66, 73-4
Theophania, 213
Theopneusty, 213
Thinker, the, 31

Thought, constructive, 123; destructive, 78, 122
Time, Wheel of, 216
Tree, fruit of, 38, 148-9; leaves of, 148; of Life, xiii, 91, 112-4, 123, 140, 164; meaning of, 116
Tree and Serpent Worship, 125
Tree of Knowledge, 114-5
Tree of Life, xiii, 91, 112-4, 123, 140, 164
Trees in the Garden, Chapter x, 109
Triangle, reflected, 150-1
Twain One Flesh, Chapter xiv, 150
Types, Ideal, 34, 44-5, 67

U

Ultimates, 26
Unclean, call thou not, 159
Unity in Duality, Chapter xiii, 142
Urge, to perfection, 72, 80

V

Virgin, meaning of, 230
Voice of Isis, The, quoted, 58, 61, 83-4-5, 91, 109, 117-8, 120-4-6-9, 180-6-7, 213
Voice of the Silence, quoted, 132

W

Whale, legs of the, 20
Wheel, Mill, 216
Will, free, 118
Woman, leads husband, 157-8; mind of, 88; mission of, 90-1, 146, 157, 171; place of, 87-9, 93, 131; priestess, 91
Women, "advanced," 56-8; aping men, 92

X

X-rays, effect of, 41

Y

Yatsar, meaning of, 55

www.ingramcontent.com/pod-product-compliance
Lightning Source LLC
Chambersburg PA
CBHW061635040426
42446CB00010B/1435